I'll Die
After
Bingo

I'll Die After Bingo

The Unlikely Story of My Decade as a Care Home Assistant

POPE LONERGAN

EBURY
SPOTLIGHT

1 3 5 7 9 10 8 6 4 2

Ebury Press, an imprint of Ebury Publishing
20 Vauxhall Bridge Road
London SW1V 2SA

Ebury Press is part of the Penguin Random House
group of companies whose addresses can be found at
global.penguinrandomhouse.com

Penguin
Random House
UK

First published by Ebury Press in 2022

www.penguin.co.uk

A CIP catalogue record for this book is
available from the British Library

ISBN 9781529109337

Printed and bound in Great Britain by Clays Ltd, Elcograf S.p.A.
Imported into the EEA by Penguin Random House Ireland, Morrison
Chambers, 32 Nassau Street, Dublin D02 YH68.

The events described in this book are based on the experiences of the author. To preserve patient confidentiality and the privacy of individuals, details relating to places, locations and events have been changed as have the names and other identifying features of people. Any similarities are purely coincidental. This is because this is not a book about the individuals, places and events described but about what we can learn from them and how they shape our approach as carers of the elderly and of each other.

To the 12 centimetres of my small intestine that were cut out of me in 2016. Because of you I won an argument with a girl I went on a date with. It was about who'd had the most intestine removed. She only lost 9 centimetres. Pathetic.

CONTENTS

PROLOGUE

There's a small stage, illuminated by a single spotlight – and inside that circle is a wooden bar stool. Directly in front of the stool is a microphone in a stand. The cable snakes off into the surrounding black, and a thick black curtain provides the backdrop just behind the stage. If you look closely enough, you'll notice the mud and the dust at the curtain's frayed edges, a couple of shoe prints on the dusty wooden stage, and even a woodlouse scaling the steep vertical leg of the stool. This is what theatre director Peter Brook referred to as 'the rough space': informal, even dirty. An intimate environment that lends itself to honest, semi-pathological disclosure.

A man walks onto the stage. He's six foot one with a shaved head and beaded sweat covering his scalp. He has an oval face, a slightly protruding Neanderthal brow, thick eyebrows, a structured nose, and small, deep-set eyes with long eyelashes. His angular jawline is covered by a patchy beard – unkempt, unmaintained. He looks kind of old – except when he smiles, tugging his sweatshirt so it doesn't cling to his protruding belly.

'My dad says I've finally caught up with my body dysmorphia,' he says off-handedly, into the microphone.

He smiles again. A broad smile, revealing an open face, with apple cheeks and dimples, and white-ish teeth (though the bottom row is crooked and, on the top row, one of the incisors has a chip in it). The smile also causes one of his eyes to wince. And, for the first time, it's apparent he has crow's feet.

His torso is squat and barrel-shaped, with fat gathered on his belly, his hips and what were formerly his pectorals. He's in a sweatshirt embroidered with a cartoon of two male clowns entertaining an audience of geriatrics (with walking frames to convey their age) seated in a crescent formation – though one of the empty chairs has tipped onto its side. There are balloons and party banners. The text on one of the banners reads 'The Care Home Tour'.

The sleeves of the sweatshirt are bunched up around his elbows, revealing thin forearms and glass wrists. Basketball shorts (black, with a white vertical stripe) show off his long, skinny legs (a curse of genetics). And these are partially covered by black socks, which have been pulled up to the bottom of his shins. The final item of clothing to make up this ensemble: black trainers, emblazoned with the same brand logo as the socks and the shorts.

Onstage, he stands upright, with a wide stance and his duck feet pointing outwards. (He's extremely flat-footed.) The backs of his wrists press into his love handles, and his hands, replicating his feet, also point away from the body. Taken in its entirety, the posture is like that of a two-handled teapot.

He has a subtle lisp, a noticeable Essex accent, and a voice that sounds as if it's been partially filtered through his nose. He describes it as a 'blobby, lumpy voice'. A colleague – a fellow comedian – once said he was 'someone who's intelligent but *sounds* thick'.

A subtle, barely audible hum emanates from the darkness – and then stops. Like an old hard drive briefly returning to life. He pulls the microphone cable across the stage, sending up a small cloud of dust, and sits on the stool. He plants his right foot on the floor to stabilise his top-heavy body. The left leg is bent at the knee and his sole presses into the stool's foot railing.

Again, he pinches his sweatshirt and pulls it away from his stomach.

'So, there you go. Anyway, I should probably introduce myself ...'

• • •

I'm Pope Lonergan. I'm a stand-up comedian, Quaker, (recovering) drug addict and lifelong Essex boy. (Apart from a small hiatus in Pompey.)

For nearly a decade I've also worked as a care assistant, or support worker, or carer. (You can use these interchangeably.) There hasn't been a conscious passing of the occupational torch. But Mum, her sister and their mum have all worked as nurses, or demoted themselves to 'care assistant' to balance the job with raising young children. And they've done this their entire working lives.

The term 'wiping arses' has become a stand-in for the entire field of social care – especially elder care. It's one task of many performed on the job, but wiping an arse ('wearing their haemorrhoid as a cufflink') seems to represent not only abjection and waste but also the status of the people who are carrying out these duties; the misconception (perpetuated, unfortunately, by other medical staff) that they're unskilled, uncaring and unprofessional. It's mucky work. 'Grunt's work'. But work that 'just needs to be done'. And because this was/is the public image of the care profession, for me, it wasn't a calling – merely a matter of convenience. (I needed a job and my cousin knew someone.)

Upon taking that first job – and, later, others in the various care homes I've worked in nationally, all full of elderly people with different levels of capacity – I found out that, yes, there are slack, dishonoured bodies (and minds), there's bodily spillage, and somatic degradation – incontinence pads swollen with piss, and iron-rich stools plugging up intestines – but there's also tenderness, and love, and a delicacy of feeling. Ablution rituals that are tinged with a form of divinity. Compulsive repetition and lemniscate pathways that uncover some essential truth about the world. Brutal, pitch-black comedy and nutty absurdist theatre. Care ethics, cooperation, holistic humanism, interdependency – people helping people.

I've always thought that telling embarrassing stories onstage, and working through my own shameful experiences in front of an audience, allows the listener to forgive themselves for whatever caused them to feel shame. And in that same vein I believe unsanitised, and unsentimentalised, representations of ageing can be used to highlight our universality and extract the shame from dementia.

What else can we do? Pretend it isn't happening? If you want to deny the person with dementia's lived experience to accord with the figment of them you hold in your head – an image of what they *used* to be – it's as if you're implying that, in their current state, they should be brushed under the carpet or dumped with the rest of the clinical waste (which is actually how the painter Francis Bacon wanted to be discarded: 'When I'm dead, put me in a plastic bag and throw me in the gutter').

Unfortunately, this *is* what happens – not only to the residents themselves but to the entire industry. It's seen as lowly and inconvenient, as something to hide away. And because of this, social care is deprived of time, energy, investment – and, worst of all, dignity and due consideration.

As I've mentioned, I'm a recovering drug addict. For years I was boiling up fentanyl patches, or swigging oxycodone from Coke cans, or necking 60 dihydrocodeine tablets in one go. Though not like the hedonistic party boys of comedy;* I was getting high and attending Quaker meetings. I was a recluse. But I warmed to care work, and found solace within care homes, because I recognised we (people with mental health problems and our wider network of support) are all being relegated to society's margins. And being on both sides of the curtain (*behind* and *in front of* a mental health disorder), I intuitively understood that connecting with the person behind the illness, while dodging sinkholes in a dilapidating social care sector – there are ways of doing it that bring colour back to the recipient's life.

I've been variously described as 'captivating', 'nauseating', 'rambunctious', 'gloriously horrid' and 'heart-stoppingly raw'. I'm an 'Essex Desperate', cheeky yet in pain. A comedian who also does care work. A care worker who also does comedy. Addicted to drugs, books and anything else that gives me a temporary release. And the people I'm working with, the people I'm caring for, are just as multi-faceted and many-dimensioned as me and the rest of us.

Some of the main themes I'll be exploring here under the rubric of 'care work', and as an individual that's exempt from

* They won't let me come on their podcasts. Even if I promise to bring booze. And pay them.

the social milieu of the 'professional class',* are: gendered work/ caring being perceived as innately feminine; personhood; dignity in old age; profit maximisation in the social care sector; the physical toll of the job; the mental toll of the job; ageing and death; humour as a coping mechanism; what makes a good carer; being an outsider (addicts and elderly people are both, in their own ways, marginalised by society); and the balance between cruelty and kindness.

This is in no way a comprehensive or definitive account of the complex relationships, and competing needs, you'll find in more forensic studies of care work. There are plenty of them out there – which makes the lack of public attention towards the profession even more dumbfounding.

Instead, this book is a hyper-individualistic and personal account. Erratic, digressionary, crass, humane and (hopefully) a little bit funny and a little bit wise. It's an entire book of me, standing here, or at work, and banging on – until you're sick to death of me.

But, for now, I'll leave you with this:

When I walk into the care home, the first thing I see is a sign that reads 'Respect & Love for Everyone'. It's a good maxim to live your life by. Especially when you're trying to show respect for people who are in their autumnal years.

---

* They won't let me come to their dinner parties. Even if I promise to bring wine. And pay them.

First thing I see at the start of a 14-hour shift:

'Respect & Love for Everyone'.

The only problem with that is I then spend the next 14 hours … washing old knobs for minimum wage.

So – where's my fucking respect?

INTRODUCTION

AM I DEAD NOW? I FEEL QUITE DEAD.

'You're buried at the roots of a tree.'

'Wait. Say that again,' I reply.

'They want to be buried. Their body buried. But not in a coffin. Buried into the earth. At the roots ... at the roots of a big tree. And that ... and they will gradually ... make the tree bigger.'

'Well, that's quite ... that's quite a nice thought. I like that. So that you're the one who's enabling the growth of the tree.'

'Yeah,' Sylvia confirms.

'Like you're horse manure.'

'What, dear?'

'Like you're horse manure.'

'Yeah, that's right! Exactly. Yeah.'

'That's quite a nice thought. I like that. So even though you're gone, you're creating growth in something else.'

'Yeah, but the Forestry Commission condemned it.'

'Oh no.'

'They said it wasn't right.'

'Do you reckon I'll live to be as old as you, Sylvia?'

'Well, you've got a long way to go yet. Can I have some more biscuit?'

It's an hour until my shift ends. Sylvia's in bed, gumming a custard cream. We're in the gloaming and you can see the purpling skies and the setting sun in her west-facing window. This suits her because she's averse to the light. I once jokingly commented that this might make her a vampire and, after a pause, she replied, 'Pope. I think it's silly you believe in vampires. No wonder your girlfriend left you.'

In these down moments, I choose to sit in the leather reclining chair next to Sylvia's bed, with remnants of food gathered in the creases, scrolling through my phone, because the mad rush of assisting people to their own beds – the adrenaline spike of bending, hoisting, lifting, removing, wiping, empty-ing, folding, spreading, plumping, and repeat, repeat, repeat – can be exhausting. Physically arduous and mentally taxing. But with a 14-hour shift almost behind me, I've decided to break off from the world. To disconnect. It's the most relaxed I've felt all week. And because I've cared for Sylvia for so many years, we can share a comfortable silence without worrying about filling it.

'Can you answer me this?' says Sylvia, after a few minutes of contemplation.

'Yeah. What's wrong?' I reply.

'And you have to be honest with me.'

'Of course, of course.'

'Am I dead now? I feel quite dead,' she says, almost cheerfully.

'Nah. You're fine. You're not dead.'

'Oh.'

There's a pause.

'Maybe tomorrow then,' she replies.

There's another brief pause – followed by the sound of her chewing and me repositioning myself, as I continue to scroll on my phone.

CHAPTER ONE

I'm in the care home, standing on a ladder outside the ground floor's lounge. The ground floor is split into four areas where the residents' rooms are located: Harmony, Melody, Symphony and Rhapsody.

Harmony is the first section, near the front entrance (though divided by a long corridor). It's mainly 'residential' – which means a lot of the residents have been assessed as compos mentis, and not a flight risk, though they may have problems with mobility.

Each section has its own dining room and lounge. The middle two are combined – or if there's an uptick in residents who need two people to assist them, Melody is split down the middle: half the corridor goes to Harmony; half goes to Symphony. And because the elders in these sections (Melody and Symphony) have dementia, it's more secure. You have to tap in a key code to open doors. (Melody and Symphony's lounge is connected to the conservatory, which opens onto decking that covers some of the back garden.) There are residents who are more canny than we give them credit for. They hover as we're entering the code, memorise it* and then break bad/go to the garden and sit next to the goldfish pond. It's rare for them to get any further than that – but it can happen.

Rhapsody is a smaller area towards the back of the main building, mostly comprising temporary residents and those who are often in and out of hospital for routine appointments.

There are 65 bedrooms – even numbers on the right-hand side of the corridor and odd numbers on the left. (There's a total of 130 rooms in the facility, spread over three floors.) Room 32, where Sylvia resides, and from where she calls out my name whenever she hears a noise, is diagonal to where I'm currently hanging Christmas decorations.

Behind me is the medicine cupboard. It's locked. Access is limited to care team managers (who oversee all the carers working

---

* The level of memory loss in a person with dementia depends on what kind of dementia they have. If the areas of the brain responsible for memory formation aren't critically damaged, a resident with dementia can, and will, memorise these codes. Or memorise the pattern the code makes on the key pad when you're pressing the numbers. Who knows? Either way, they've retained it.

on the floor they've been assigned), visiting district nurses and the home managers – but the lock's four-digit code has been conveniently inked into a nearby spot that isn't too difficult to locate. And as a boots-and-braces safeguard against the misappropriation of controlled substances, any Schedule 2 drugs (oxycodone, fentanyl, diamorphine – all the good shit) are stored inside a safe and recorded in a controlled drugs register.

It's midday and unseasonably warm. The lounge leads to a conservatory, and soft light is pouring in through its windows. As usual, the residents have asked to keep these shut (at least until a menopausing carer forces them open again).

Bargain Hunt is on the TV. Some residents watch with interest; some natter; some shout to themselves, harassed by private inquisitions. One of them stands, in contrast to everyone else, tapping his foot and clicking his fingers to the sound of the red team deliberating on the price of a porcelain creamer. Sweet, toe-tapping nutter, travelling on his own wavelength.

'The thing, the thingy – that! That looks rubbish,' Pat shouts.

Pat's thickset and four foot twelve and could be described as matronly. The dictum 'It's much safer to be feared than loved' informs her managerial style. But she wears this identity like pantomime make-up, and the staff dutifully play the subordinates because of the 14 years she's worked as a care team manager. (CTMs dispense medication, liaise with doctors, complete mountains of paperwork and generally issue directives to us, the underlings.)

Fourteen years of seeing the same lobby, the same reception desk and the same manager's office on the right. The same sign that says 'Respect & Love for Everyone'.

Even those who are higher up the chain, such as the home manager and the deputies (one hardworking, one redundant), cautiously cede their authority to Pat. She's the Inconvenient Elder who's always done things her way, so why bother asking her to change?

We regularly hear her remark, 'If you think I'm changing, you better get your head out your arse cos I ain't changing for shit.'

'The wotsit, the thing, the tinsel! The tinsel needs to go higher. Put it up higher!' comes the next command.

'Alright, alright!' I reply, exasperated. 'I can't keep mucking about with this. I've got to help Susan with her—'

'Susan can bloody wait! I'll ask her to drink the whole bottle of Oramorph if she carries on being rude! Then let's see who's dead,' Pat barks.

'Why were you arguing about who's dead?'

'She said I was dead and I said, "How can I be dead when I'm helping you with your meds?" and *she* said, "Well if you're not dead will you hurry it along, please?"'

Pat raises her eyebrows in a kind of mock incredulousness at Susan's audacity. 'Believe that? Cheeky bloody cow.'

These are the conversations you have in the care home. Intermediate. Illogical. Straddling two timelines simultaneously. Trying to figure out the boundaries of observable reality as they shift in the mind of someone with a neurodegenerative disease. You can be dead or alive – or somewhere in the middle.

Pat's *style* extends to the residents. It sometimes makes me uncomfortable, as it's easy for others to misinterpret it, for onlookers to see it as cruelty towards a vulnerable person. Yes, there are moments when things go a step too far, and I'll intervene, adopting the role of the placid arbitrator, but there's also a familial intimacy in the home. A trust.

I once spoke to comedian Alfie Brown about saying things to my friends that border on offensive. It's like letting the belly of my id hang out. And he theorised that it's a method of cultivating, or confirming, an inherent trust within a friendship group. You can say horrible shit to your friends because you know *they* know the words aren't loaded; that they're permissible only within the capsule of your relationship.

Pat has the same bond – the acceptable-boundary-pushing bond – with everyone who works or resides in the home. She isn't always appropriate, but that's a natural part of her character, which is softened by moments of kindness that go beyond the call of duty, like when she uses her own money to buy the residents provisions that aren't supplied by the company (sweets, ice lollies, pilchards) or pulls me aside to check on my mental health or my recovery. Underlying her tough love approach is real heart and an investment in other people's well-being. We're very close. And Susan, for instance, laughs when Pat moans at her, or reciprocates with her own bit of cheekiness. It's a well-established dynamic, built on verbal sparring. And through these small acts of charity, or conversational roughhousing, I can see how Pat thinks of them, of *us*: as family.

'Put the tinsel up where I want it or I'll choke you with it!' she shouts.

After finishing with the decorations, and Pat's demands, I make my way along the corridor. We regularly have to sacrifice our breaks, so I plan on ducking into the staff bathroom opposite the dining room – a locked, cavernous space, where I can sit on the toilet and lean back on a toilet roll wedged between my head and the cistern. If you don't move, the lights go out and you're left with an eerie glow beneath the door. A meditative space. Even with the shuffle and grunt of a resident passing by. And you just hope, *pray*, they don't try the handle.

The windowless ground-floor corridor, which runs almost the entire length of the building, is painted in blues and greens. From overhead comes the hum and glare of phosphorescent light. Wooden handrails horizontally divide the walls, with scuffed corners and indentations caused by wayward trolleys.* I know it like the back of my hand.

On the walls are low-resolution print-outs in cheap plastic frames. Album covers, film posters or celebrities the elders might recognise. Scanning the images, you realise there's no

---

* Sometimes I'll purposely smash trolleys into the door frames. This is my petty way of incurring additional, avoidable, charges for the avaricious company directors to deal with.

consistency in the choices: President Lyndon B. Johnson and Premier Alexei Kosygin at the Glassboro Summit Conference; the promotional photograph for a 'Boys 1950s Fancy Dress' competition, with a modern-day boy dressed as Elvis (close enough); a press shot of Fred Elliott from *Coronation Street* opening a supermarket in Guernsey.

Further along, there's a bedroom where carers tend to quicken their step as they pass. Number 33. Inside are Louise and Edith.

Louise has a round, almost juvenile face, but she's shrunken in on herself, hunched to avoid capture or the anger of a harried carer. She's wracked with an anxiety that plugs her voice, letting out the occasional pre-empted apology that's meant to disarm but only serves to emphasise the ease with which people can swallow her up and spit her out.

Louise is Edith's daughter. Edith has dementia with Lewy bodies. She's permanently confined to her bed, where she's repositioned every two hours and assisted with all her care needs. She's a fallen fledgling wearing milk bottle glasses. A huge lesion on her head is unmissable despite her shock of white curly hair.

Louise is now highly attuned to the sound of an approaching staff member, so as soon as she hears someone coming, she pokes her head out of the door.

'Pope. Would you mind? Mum might need changing. Sorry. Very, very sorry.'

I'm not one of those carers who can leave a resident in a soiled pad without it nagging at their conscience, so, for now, I have to sacrifice my planned trip to the sensory deprivation chamber/ staff bathroom.

Sniffs and chirrups. Mumbled fragments of speech. Her face contorts and then relaxes. Her eyebrows spring upwards and the corners of her mouth ascend, a moment of amusement. These are the subtle semiotics, the language of the face, that communicate Edith's interiority. And this is what I see when I crouch beside the bed and speak to Louise *through* Edith, assuring her that her mum isn't being forgotten.

'You've eaten really well today, Edith,' I say. 'I think we were chatting about my trip to Liverpool, weren't we.'

(*We* weren't chatting about shit. It was very much me doing all the talking.)

She doesn't respond, but Louise, looking longingly at her mum's face, says, 'That's good isn't it, Mum? We've been there once or twice, haven't we?' She then turns to me and asks whether she's had open bowels today – a favourite line of enquiry.

Every day. She's here every single day, wearing a practical winter coat and carrying a plastic bag containing a banana, a notepad and a ballpoint pen – sitting in silence by her mum's bedside, trying to interpret those signs.

It gives me a pang of despair when I pass the room and see them together. Louise gently whispering consolations. Maybe she's hoping she'll alight upon the correct combination of words that'll work like a magic spell and drag Edith back from the limited world she now inhabits.

Louise has a younger sister who is a gregarious socialiser. A teacher who always visits her mum on a Saturday, and when she does she provides positive reinforcement to the carers and an easy-going cheerfulness that everyone responds to. Easy company. And when she leans against the door frame of the care team manager's office – asking the assembled carers, paperwork piled up beside them, how their work's been – she's met with a summary of her sister's obsessiveness,* fastidiousness† and anxiety.‡

Helena plays her part in the conversation and gives a knowing eye-roll at her sister's idiosyncrasies, but when she speaks to a more tolerant member of staff,§ she fleshes out the particular family dynamics.

In the past, she's revealed to me that Louise was always hiding behind her mum's apron. That never went away. Her whole life was, *is*, her mum. While Helena and their brother, Alan, grew up and had families, Louise stayed looking after their mum until she came here.

Gently rubbing the tips of her fingers together and shifting weight from one foot to the other, Louise stutters, 'I did a bit of research into … I couldn't see any information online …'

---

* 'Two drops of urine, Helena. I'm not gonna change her pad for two drops of urine.'
† 'Why is she brushing her hair *again*, Helena? I've seen more hair on a mouse's bollocks.'
‡ 'I was ten minutes late with her Tramadol and I thought she was gonna vomit. Ain't that right, girls? We thought she was gonna fucking vomit.'
§ Me. I'm a saint.

She reaches for her coat and from the pocket pulls out a card and something in a plastic bag. She hands them to me.

'You know, I always say I wouldn't know what I'd do without …'

She lets the sentence hang.

'Anyway, thank you, Pope, for everything you do for Mum. Merry Christmas. And I'm sorry if Quakers aren't allowed grapes.'

I like Louise. For her the world is made up of jagged edges to be avoided, and I have a lot of patience for people who struggle to navigate their way through existence.

I've spent the majority of my life feeling insecure about whether I fit in, what I look like and if I'm being judged for the things I say. The normal vicissitudes of Being, whether it's trying to establish affectional bonds or staving off debilitating self-doubt. I know this isn't particularly novel. (An insecure comedian? Nah, never! I don't believe it!)

But as insecure people are usually equipped with a kind of radar for other insecure people, marginal, maladapted figures have always come into my orbit.

Being so hyper-conscious of myself, and excavating my own emotional difficulties, has always helped me to wear the acne'd skin of other people's insecurities; to know something about their inner lives. Maybe it's because, knowing what a fucking mare it can be just to step outside and start the day, I try to practise the little gestures of kindness and civility that can make the transition from inside (the inner realm) to outside (the social realm) more bearable.*

'Sorry to keep asking about Mum's bowels,' Louise says. 'You know I'd rather check in with you than the others. I'm glad you understand. I've never known how to *do* people.'

We're by Edith's bedside, each of us holding one of her frail hands – all tendons and weakening pulse. She's unable to contribute in any substantial way, but whenever she makes a noise or action that seems to be in sync with our conversation – a fleeting smile or an evanescent 'lovely' – we're effusive in our recognition of her offering.

I know, or I assume, it's the residue of a once-brimming cognition. Thoughts of Devon or the smell of churches or the claustrophobia of a post-partum girdle. But Louise thinks it's reanimation, rejuvenation; that she's coming back. Rather this than granules of her self being poured into the ether.

I've never known how to *do* people either – at least not without the lubrication of alcohol or the glue of dependency (a glue that can be suffocating). Having been part of the comedy industry for a few years now, I've realised stand-up isn't an inherently collaborative form. Comedians are hyper-individualistic, entrepreneurial and self-reliant. Selfish egomaniacs, mostly – with a gladiatorial, competitive edge. I'm also part of a boisterous family. During a recent get-together, my brother and I squared

---

* Oof. This is too close to 'self-care literature' for my liking. My main bit of advice is this: start fights to calm down. Street fights. That'll sort it.

up to each other while arguing about who had the biggest beard in March 2010.*

I'm no stranger to overt displays of power and status – even the low-stakes power of beard fullness. But sometimes you want to relinquish your ego and attend to the needs of someone like Edith, or provide emotional support to someone like Louise, rather than achieve recognition, and a transitory sense of worth, from the communal response of an audience.

To me, applying moisturiser to the hollow of Edith's clavicle to prevent flakes of dry skin from building up, like a mound of vanquished butterflies, or letting Louise know how alert she was to the sound of my voice during breakfast, that, to me, is the best way of *doing* people.†

I leave Edith's room and carry on to the care team manager's office at the corridor's midpoint. It's 2pm. Time for the change-over between the early shift and the late shift.

'Oh, look. A tiny little baby,' I hear from over my shoulder.

Barry's a resident who's known for his extreme fluctuations in mood. From twinkly-eyed conviviality to explosive physical aggression. And when this switch occurs, and he's intent on breaking free of imagined constraints, it's difficult to appease him. In old photos he has a tall, brawny labourer's build, similar to Fred West's, and the jutting jaw of a man who's used to leading with his chest. But now, in his twilight years, he's diminished.

---

* I did. Fuck you, Ben.

† Though please don't take audiences away from me.

Hunched over, his top half protrudes forward like his jawline. An assertiveness, a dominant mien, still lingers in his head. And in these moments of agitation, that's how he conceives of himself. But to us, to those who fully inhabit the present, he's seen as obstreperous. And I hate that. I hate that his old self has slipped away, beyond his grasp.

Once, when I assisted him in removing his soiled clothing (one of his main triggers – because of the dual indignity of soiling himself and of being seen in this state by another man), he reacted violently. So now when he needs assisting, I make it seem as if he's guiding the situation. Like he's the foreman.

'OK. So these are pretty mucky,' I usually say, pointing at the pants and trousers, 'What do you reckon we should do with them?'

Then his anger subsides.

'OK, OK,' he normally replies, gathering his thoughts. Then in a calm, temperate voice, 'To me, and if I'm being totally honest with myself, this here looks like shit. Yes. Shit. This is shit. So it's probably best – and tell me if I'm wrong here – it's probably best if we bin 'em.'

He can be lovely, too, of course! One of his favourite jokes is to point at a small porcelain house – one of those ornaments that appeared out of nowhere – and pretend it is, in fact, *his* house. One of our recent conversations went like this:

'I'm a big Barry and that's a little house. How's a big Barry going to fit in a little house? Little house. Big Barry.' He cried with laughter.

Proper belly laughs.

'It'd be a bit of a struggle, wouldn't it,' I replied, infected by his unbridled gaiety.

'When I killed my wife in that house,' he retorted, now sober and severe, 'that was the real struggle.'

And that quickly terminated that bit of repartee.

As far as I know, he never killed his wife, but thus is the nature of dementia.

'It's all lost. It's a lost little baby,' I hear Barry say, and catch him out the corner of my eye shuffling into Edith's room with a questioning look on his face, hands in his pockets, and a Father Christmas hat on his head.

Thankfully, Louise is aware of Barry's temper, his reluctance to take direction from other people and how hard it is to discern what, exactly, makes Barry erupt on such occasions. I notice Louise feverishly ball the air between her fingers and hide her mum's special plastic spoons.

'Hello there, Barry,' she says. 'How are you feeling today? Mum's actually sleeping so I don't think you should—'

'It's OK, little baby. With your little baby head,' comes Barry's response, with no acknowledgement of Louise's presence, as he shuffles closer to the bed.

Barry reaches out his huge, heavy hands, with knuckles like ancient knots, gently places the tips of his fingers on Edith's scalp, and starts squeezing as if he were releasing a bit of air from the head of a doll.

Louise, stricken, unable to move, quietly begins hyperventilating.

Barry gently squeezes while Edith's mouth forms an 'O' shape and emits a sound similar to a tawny owl's mating call. It's upbeat, surprised.

'Small little head she's got,' he says, smiling, noticing Louise for the first time, and experiencing a bout of Good Barry – Good, Kindly Barry. 'Small like a button. Little button head.'

I can see Louise is close to vomiting.

Trying to manage different needs, and the competing demands on your time, is part of the skill of being a good care assistant. Even when you're putting up Christmas decorations, you're worrying about Susan or trying to appease your manager. Then you gently guide Barry away from his triggers – a geriatric Buckeroo – while simultaneously preventing him from popping Edith's head. *Then* there are the family members, the district nurses, the paramedics …

This isn't an unusual day.

• • •

The care team manager's office is a long, narrow room with two windows overlooking the main corridor and the garden. In it are rows of care plans (files that reduce each resident down to vital statistics, medical histories and succinct observation records); filing cabinets; drawers stuffed with old paperwork and knick-knacks; a whiteboard that's used for daily reminders. Today it reads 'Don't leave shampoo with Dorothy'.*

The space operates as a salon or coffeehouse in that it's exposed to the traffic of the corridor, so it's part of the public sphere – with itinerant residents and their visiting family members occasionally turning up with grievances to air or suggestions to make. But when the door's closed we're free to indulge ourselves and talk with impunity. *To let the belly of our id hang out.*

But today one of the carer's children is sitting in the corner, waiting for his mum to finish her shift.

'I'm getting dinosaurs for Christmas,' he tells me.

'Yes, he's getting dinosaurs for Christmas, Pope,' Pat confirms, sitting at her desk by the viewing window, giving me a pained look. 'And he's told me that ...'

Pat lowers her voice and speaks out the side of her mouth.

'... sixteen fucking times already.'

'Ah, dinosaurs!' I exclaim. 'I hope you've got your dinosaur-wrangling licence!'

I lean back, push my chest forward, and pat my belly twice in quick succession. It's a kind of dad pose, a way of creating a clear demarcation between adult and child. Self-assured and gently authoritative.

'I'm getting real ones! Real dinosaurs!' he replies.

----
* Dorothy drank some shampoo.

'If you were getting real dinosaurs I think you'd be dead within thirty seconds, wouldn't you,' Pat interjects, looking at me and rolling her eyes. 'So don't say stupid things.'

He goes quiet.

I was a happy kid, though shy and plagued by insecurity.

Mum often had to collect me from primary school for various reasons. Like the time one of my classmates tipped me off about Saddam Hussein's imminent nuclear attack. Or when I was disturbed by tales of a 'clitoris tree' courtesy of a prematurely sexualised nine-year-old called Greg, who'd sourced some of the correct information about adult sexuality and, in his innocence, re-contextualised it.

A key thing I do remember from my childhood was my parents stressing to me the sanctity of all living things. From them I'd like to think that I have acquired the necessary quality of any good carer: the capacity to provide care and tenderness. At least some of the time.

For the majority of her career Mum has worked as an auxiliary nurse and, while I was in primary school, she worked for ten years as a care assistant to accommodate my and my brother's school schedule.

I don't know if I consciously gravitated towards care to follow in Mum's footsteps. She never made it sound particularly appealing. As a child I mainly associated care work with Mum's impatience after she'd returned from a shift, and work shoes that stank like shit. Although, I knew there were patients that left an indelible mark on her – and for those, her heart still swells when she recalls their struggles. (But in a recent chat, she admitted to me she can't remember much about most of the elders she cared for. Only vague details, like they're the textual remains of antiquity, lost to time. Isn't that sad? All those sparks of connection; all those little asides and inside jokes. Dead and gone.)

Dad was a detective (with a drug addict son*), but he's since retrained as a senior-school maths teacher. Prior to tearing his ACL, he'd played rugby since college. He's also a keen gardener. Our garden has always been an environment teeming with vibrant matter; I think it provided Dad with a haven away from work more than the family did. If people ask him about his old cases, like the Essex Boys murders, his stock response is, 'A lot of it was just paperwork and horrible bastards.'

So when I was younger, Mum and Dad both had jobs that occasionally pushed them close to the dark extremes of human behaviour. Like in the eighties and early nineties when my mum worked alongside my nanny Vera and aunty Val (Mum's sister) at the burns unit in Billericay Hospital, where she witnessed the horrifying sight of a toddler with third-degree burns. The parents were suspected of, and later charged with, putting her in a scalding-hot bath. Mum said the worst part was being asked to make them a drink. They hadn't been arrested yet, but the police were there and the staff were told what might have happened. But she had to be professional and take them coffee.

---

* You fucked that one up, Mark!

In my experience too, visitors to the care home don't always have the residents' best interests at heart, and it's something we as carers really have to watch out for. For instance, when Susan first arrived, she was brought in by her twin daughters, but there was a 'cousin' who'd visit separately.

Susan suffered with dementia as well as paralysis on the right side of her body. ('I'm right-handed, you know. God's having a laugh.') She'll often forget what has transpired moment to moment, and repeat the same series of questions over and over again ('Where's my daughter? Am I safe?'). But despite this, and the interminability of such repetition, I've developed a close relationship with her. She'll remark on how reassured she is by my presence. And even though she can't always identify who I am in relation to her, she's committed my face and my name to memory, and she knows she's safe with me and that she can relax while I'm on shift.

Having established a bond with her early on, I was instantly weary of this big-faced, overly chummy man* whose unfailingly polite demeanour seemed to mask a manipulative and coercive nature. If he was visiting, he'd often speak on Susan's behalf when we addressed her, or he'd assist her with food and drink even though she was capable of using her left arm for such tasks (and we were supposed to encourage independence when necessary). It was almost like he wanted her to need him. On

---

* Imagine a fat pantomime dame with all the make-up hosed off. That's what he looked like. He creeped me out.

occasion, you glimpsed how she must have been in her younger days: assertive, sociable, with a wicked sense of humour. But when this 'cousin' was around she was lost and seeking guidance from him. And I'd notice his little flare-ups of anger if she resisted his help.

It turned out, according to the daughters, that he *was* genuinely her cousin, but he hadn't seen her for years prior to the worsening of her health issues. He was also a convicted con man who'd 'reconnected' with Susan while she was in this weakened state and was now occupying her house, refusing to leave. Eventually we were directed not to allow him entry into the home and, over time, the memory of him snagged on a stick and floated away in the slipstream of time. Susan forgot about him. But before the full story was revealed to us – when we were documenting his suspicious behaviour without it being confirmed – we had to maintain a professional disposition and offer him tea and biscuits like he was any other visitor. ('I hope he fucking chokes on it,' Pat would whisper, as he bit into a ginger nut.)

We're still close, Susan and I. She's one of five Susans I care for – so I refer to her as Susan H. She has a husky, fag ash voice, effectively utilised when screaming through a regular bout of tears, letting combative carers know they're a 'Wicked fucking bitch!'

She has dark, leathery skin, an oval face and eyes that are close together. Her hair (short and sensible, but cursed with the ruptured swirls of untameable cow's licks) is flecked with black and grey. On the back of her neck is a weeping crater, as if a small mine has been detonated. And this, in turn, has been landlocked by thick, rippling scar tissue. It's a wound caused by years of compulsive 'picking'. After various rounds of anti-histamines, steroid injections, etc., a conclusion hasn't been reached on whether it's psychological or physiological.

In care homes there's an aggressive spotlight on corporeality, on maladies and ailments. People can be squeamish about such brutal aesthetics or bodily functions, but I want these things to become – to a certain extent – socialised. Or, at the very least, accepted as a fundamental part of being human.

I have a high tolerance for 'body stuff'. After one of my childhood Chicken Little episodes, afraid of bombs and Middle Eastern dictators (things that regularly encroached on my day-to-day life), I was picked up from school and taken to the care home where Mum was on a shift. There was an Easter raffle on. Much like today, the homes then were underfunded due to the prioritisation of profit extraction by company directors. With such a diminished 'entertainment' budget, you were only in with a chance of winning either *Jerry Maguire* on VHS, a sweaty cake or some leftover nutrition shakes.

Mum managed to get a tin for me to store my Pogs, which were these little plastic or cardboard discs with pictures printed on the front that every school kid collected in the early nineties. The tin was baby blue, with a friendly bunny embossed onto the lid. It was a nice surprise and I did the usual appreciative gestures.

After Mum handed it to me, I removed the lid and inside was – a pile of brown sick. Or faeces. Or it may have been faecal vomit from someone with intestinal obstruction. It was obviously an oversight on my mum's part. And I quickly replaced the lid before Mum clocked it.

This was the first time I recognised, in the words of Mikhail Bakhtin (from *Rabelais and His World*), 'the grotesque image of the body'.

Afterwards I rinsed out the tin – but I remember being aware that Mum had thought of me, that she'd been excited to give me this tin, and I didn't want her to feel ashamed that it happened to be full of sick. That her present to me was, in fact, a big tin of sick. And rather than drawing attention to that fact, to the social taboo of vomit (or whatever it was), I decided to prevent Mum from feeling embarrassed by smiling, and thanking her, and cleaning it up myself, without her ever knowing.

Pogs and faecal vomit – my initiation into a slightly shitty world and finding a way to tolerate it to protect another person's feelings. That's basically care work in a nutshell, son.

• • •

I usually do 14-hour shifts – double shifts – but today I'm on an early. After talking dinosaurs, and being part of the handover (a rundown of vital information: 'Keep an eye on Barry as he's wandering into Edith's room'; 'Susan's had her Oramorph'; 'Louise's in,' said with a sigh), I walk towards the front entrance and into room 2, my last check of the day. There, I tend to an old boy named Simon. He often tells me about the war. He's 98 years old, without dementia, and has a penchant for whisky. He sleeps in Y-fronts and a vest because in the Navy they were told if the boat sinks, pyjamas weigh you down. He is small and crooked with a splashy, sibilant voice caused by a lisp. And this adds to his general gnome-ish demeanour: he's a warm, loving, grateful man whose cheerfulness prevents him from being engulfed by great reserves of melancholy.

'I remember when we were hit by the other boys,' he tells me, commencing an unprompted reminiscence while I kneel in front of him, putting on his socks. 'There was a huge crater in the side of the ship. And we were doing what we had to do. We knew our training. But I looked over to the left and my friend, my best friend, was melted. He was melted onto the side of the ship. His face was stuck to it, melted like ice cream.'

His eyes glisten with tears; the throb of a memory that has opened up right in front of him, as vibrant as the first time he witnessed it. This traumatising event must have echoed throughout his life, even 80 years after the fact.

'That's really shit,' I say, unable to summon an adequate response.

Simon is tactile and affectionate – he calls me 'darling' even though I'm another man, with a beard. So I carefully hold the tips of his arthritic fingers. He is one of the elders I want to have physical contact with, whether that be a hug, a firm pat on the shoulder or a gentle bout of 'laddin' it up'. Without being too patronising, especially to a man who lived through an era that, in some ways, was like the end of the world – Simon's a sweetheart.

'What a shit ol' death,' I conclude. Flippant, colloquial. A regretful summation of a war hero's demise. But sometimes you struggle to find the words. And, to be fair, melting *is* a shit ol' death.

These stories of unimaginable horror can come out of nowhere during a working day. I mean, it's a rare bit of candour about wartime experiences – the restless dead and secret atrocities usually remain in the steel trove of that generation's recollections – but they crop up from time to time. This one by Simon is especially evocative. It highlights that the best carers embrace the relational aspect of the job, and understand that the cultivation of these relationships can be a strong source of satisfaction for both the resident and for themselves.

It's a tragic anecdote (could have done with a couple of jokes), but Simon's willingness to confide in me, to impart this painful memory, something he may not have disclosed for a long, long time – *that's* how you achieve satisfaction in an often thankless job.

CHAPTER TWO

IS EVERYONE HAVING A SAFE AFTERNOON, LADIES AND GENTLEMEN?

For most carers (whether paid or unpaid), waking up and confronting the day can be a challenge. It's that moment where you emerge from dream time and realise you're about to be laden with any number of physically and mentally demanding tasks, often involving hostile and thankless residents. Even while I'm asleep, work often plagues me. I've dreamed of elders somnambulating across lava lakes while red-tinged urine rains from the sky. Or rows of empty, sentient wheelchairs tilting towards a giant bedpan, peering over the horizon.

My eyes open. It's still dark outside but the upper atmosphere is salmon and indigo. Tie-dyed.

I get up, no mucking about,* and instantly make my bed. As soon as I arrive at work, I'll assist the residents with washing and dressing, escort them to the dining room and, finally, the pièce de résistance, make *their* beds.

It might sound a bit strange, but achieving the satisfying geometry, and the immaculacy, of a well-made bed – and by someone with a fussy eye for particularity – it's a job I take a lot of pride in. It has a similar quality to kintsugi, the Japanese art of putting broken pottery back together again, although kintsugi embraces – even glorifies – flaws and imperfections by using gold to draw attention to the cracks. I, on the other hand, am trying to erase the tangle of sheets or the flakes of dead skin gathered in the creases by stripping and changing the bedclothes and restoring the whole thing to its previous condition – only for it to be messed up again at night-time. It's an art, bed-making. And so is changing an incontinence pad. It's a shame the clean pad and clean bed are then spoiled by a leaking elder. But this pride, this satisfaction, in the presentation of the care home environment is in stark contrast to the dump 'n' run approach of *some* of the lazy pricks I have encountered over the course of working in care homes. They'll even throw a duvet over damp urine stains.

---

* This is a puritanical attitude I've inherited from my dad: I believe waking up past 8.30 is an indulgence and that anyone who does it is a slug. (Unless they've been on night shifts. Or they're currently in a coma. Although even then they should try harder to shake it off.)

US Navy Admiral William H. McRaven delivered a famous commencement speech to a Texas university in which he stated the importance of bed-making: 'If you wanna change the world, start off by making your bed. If you make your bed every morning, you will have accomplished the first task of the day. It will give you a small sense of pride and it will encourage you to do another task. And then another. And then another.' This ethos appeals to the part of me that hopes to impress my dad. It fosters a masculinity that's straight-backed, cinched in and coloured between the lines. Dutiful and full of integrity. Unstained by a madness that spills over the rim of your being. And it speaks to the part of me that wants to lead a healthy, fresh-air existence without having to abuse drugs to leave the house.

● ● ●

It's 6.25am. The air is crisp, and pink-rimmed clouds move across the sky in the east. It's that weird point on a Sunday morning when minimum-wage employees* heading to work cross paths with the dregs of the previous night's shenanigans: the comedown kids trying to find shelter before the sun has fully risen.

---

* For a Sunday shift I'm paid £1 extra per hour. And my hourly rate is the minimum wage. I usually work 42 hours per week (three 14-hour shifts) and I'm on most Sundays (unless I'm gigging on the Saturday), but other carers are contractually obliged to work two weekends per month. One on, one off. I have migrant colleagues who work 70–82 hours per week.

I used to be one of those kids, wandering from house to house in the early morning to see which dealers were still awake. That was in my university days. I'd attend raves as they were an excuse to indulge my then totally out-of-control substance abuse. (At the time, my appearance fluctuated between Lord of Dogtown, all tanned and handsome, and Rasputin in a wifebeater and a dressing gown.) After a short-lived period of sobriety, and a move back home to focus on my dissertation (while commuting from Essex to Portsmouth four days a week), I levelled up from 'party drugs' to opioid painkillers in 2014, soon after graduating.

I get on the number 3 bus along with a Polish labourer. Prior to its arrival, he fell asleep while standing up. I notice the crushed empty cans of Tyskie in his rucksack and the one long fingernail on his little finger (which can be used to scoop cocaine out of a baggie). As I travel to work, a part of me dreading the shift ahead, I reflect on the five-year period when life gradually, incrementally, ground to a halt due to my frantic need for opiates. I'm flooded with the memory of sitting behind a locked door, perched on the toilet seat, with a piece of blue roll spread over my knees, and the crackle of a blister pack as I emptied 60 dihydrocodeine tablets onto my lap.

Oxycodone and Diet Coke. Boiled fentanyl patches. Even just over-the-counter opiates if that's what it took to top me off. I know the numbers off by heart: 10 mg of oxycodone (liquid) and up to 120 mg for slow-release tablets. (There are ways around that slow-release mechanism.) Only 12.8 mg of codeine phosphate without a prescription. Pathetic. I'm getting euphoric even thinking about it. It reminds me of being in rehab, trading war stories in the kitchen while one of the other 'service users' chewed on a teabag for a caffeine boost. Our pupils dilating, fingers jittery.

I'm an addict. Or – to use the correct medical parlance – a filthy junkie bastard. There were warning signs when I was little (single-mindedly building up my wrestling figure collection), and, if you subscribe to the 'genetic predisposition' view of substance use disorder, there was also the fact that my grandad had a gambling problem and Mum had her battles with drink. I was always going to find an outlet for my addictive tendency, so I'm not blaming the job for this.

But when I was in the midst of active addiction and we were massively overstretched due to inadequate staffing levels, thus creating working conditions that weren't only hazardous but properly dangerous – it accelerated my drug use. And I started to notice the signs of dependence throughout the work force. Carers rinsing their own supply of painkillers. The copious amounts of Monster, Diet Coke and coffee consumed as people rushed through an unending list of tasks. Overhearing the squink of a vodka cap from inside the toilet cubicle connected to the staffroom, followed by a gulp and a sharp intake of breath.

But, no, I've been clean(ish) since 2017 and I can't waste another five years of my life spacing out in a shoebox flat that smells like mince (one I shared with my ex-girlfriend) or sitting in the park next to a war memorial, shouting out football tips to junior Sunday league players. I'm finally *present* and part of the world again – but in a way that isn't alienating.

I remember reading an essay by Simone Weil – who is one of my all-time idols (along with wrestler Mick Foley, comedians Andy Kaufman and Hans Teeuwen and philosopher Walter Benjamin) – where she wrote about the powerful energy and agency of our attention. 'Attention, taken to its highest degree, is the same thing as prayer,' she says. 'It presupposes faith and love. Absolutely unmixed attention is prayer.' In care work it's so important to abandon the reward cycle, the chase for an invigorating upswing, and to relinquish your ego as much as possible. To direct your attention to the person you're caring for. When I was still using, I'd manically traipse up and down corridors in my steel-toe boots, sweaty and grey, delivering Brexit updates to people who still thought Harold Wilson was prime minister. But now I'm drug-free. I'm open, mentally alert and active – without giving all my colleagues anxiety.

I drum my fingers on the bus window. The journey is only about 25 minutes long. Then it's a 30-minute walk from the bus stop to the village where I work (population: 2,096). After arriving at the bus stop, before setting off for the care home, I speak to the homeless guy with fast-thinning hair who's built an inside-out dorm room by the post office. He has a crate he uses as a bookshelf, plus a solar-powered book light, a mound of grotty blankets and a thin sleeping bag that he ties around his waist if he's on the move. (When I was still drinking, I got pissed with him once after a long shift. He said the Jordan Peterson book *12 Rules for Life*, a manual for broken boys with a libertarian bent, changed his life – then poured more vodka into an empty tomato soup can.)

The walk is always rejuvenating, opening up hundreds of dormant gateways in my brain, and even though it usually means I'm 25 minutes late to my shift – missing most of the CTM's handover – I wouldn't sacrifice it for anything.

It's hard to convince my manager that it doesn't matter if I'm late because I'm a better, more attentive carer when I've been walking for half an hour; that being present doesn't necessarily mean you're *present*. (It's even harder to convince her not to dock my pay by 25 minutes.) Whenever I try to make the case for accommodating people's natural rhythms – a means of optimising their job performance or, when it comes to the residents, making it easier to encourage them to do an hour of exercise per day – I use my walk to work, and the increased energy and vigour I get from it, as support for my argument. It's all part of person-centred/relationship-centred care: gaining insight into patients' private experience by paying attention to when they're at their most receptive.

I arrive at the care home at 7.25am. I punch in the code to gain entry and notice there's a new sign advertising a Christmas fete, taking place the following Saturday (December 22nd). The sun is just starting to make its appearance. Soon it will be all white light and radiance. Birds chirruping. I'm sweaty (and probably will be for the remainder of the shift) but, after the walk, my spirit is slightly elevated, and I've forgotten about the low-level dread.

'Pope. Ethel's leg's burst. I know you've just got in but can you help the night staff clean it up?' asks the CTM as soon as I walk through the door.

Now I've *truly* arrived at work. After cleaning and applying a dressing to Ethel's venous leg ulcer, I go to the toilet before catching the end of the handover. In one of my favourite books, Jean-Philippe Toussaint's *The Bathroom*, the protagonist chooses to spend most of his time in the bathroom so he can, to paraphrase Henri Bergson, reshape his life into a self-repeating mechanism. The same thing, day in, day out. A life condensed. But sitting here, staring at the mirror opposite the toilet, at my reflection, and the small outbreak of acne around my hairline – I anticipate this will be one of the few times today that the grasping needs of others won't intrude on my thoughts.

The freedom I felt on my morning walk – observing the fields of daffodils as I went by – has already subsided. There's no getting away from the intense physical demands and dangers of a care occupation. According to a University of Massachusetts study,* care workers face injury rates that are more than twice as high as those of construction workers. With the combined physiological

---

* Kurowski et al. 'Changes in ergonomic exposures of nursing assistants after the introduction of a safe resident handling program in nursing homes' in *International Journal of Industrial Ergonomics*, November 2012.

and psychological effects of long work hours, night shifts, heavy lifting and other types of exertion, and the potential for exposure to blood-borne pathogens – or even verbal and physical assault from some residents – it can be a hazardous work environment.

And as I'm currently the only male carer working on the ground floor, the heavy-duty labour – the kneeling, the squatting, the raised arms, the flexed trunk, the twisting, the lifting – is usually left for me. It's an uneven distribution of labour, but I have to be fine with it because I'm a man. The *only* man. Granted, we have hoists, and slide sheets, and all the other moving and handling equipment to make it easier (and safer) for us and the residents, but there's still a lot of physical exertion involved – and pressures to cut corners. I'm only 28 but my coccyx always aches, and my right shoulder has dropped. My brother (who works as a strength and conditioning coach) said I have the tightest hamstrings he's ever seen, so my legs are permanently bent at the knees.

But I continue to work here, despite the physical and mental toll, to supplement my stand-up income, which, as with any other freelance job, is precarious and unreliable. You build a 'wage' in a piecemeal fashion: £100 for a weekend middle spot; £120 for a couple of boutique comedy shows; £400 for radio work; £300 for a Christmas show; £1,200 from the festival circuit. And if the gig goes badly, or it turns out you've been booked for the children's tent at a small festival in Kent (in a routine about shoving soap up my anus, I changed the word 'anus' to 'bum' to make it more kid-friendly), you pay back some of this with your self-esteem.

There are many (tenuous) links between being a care worker and being a stand-up comedian, but here's one that pertains to the gentle marshalling of 'awkward' geriatrics: care workers mobilise people – who may move unexpectedly, who are often unstable on their feet or cannot walk at all, who are not standard sizes or shapes, and who may not be compliant because of a difficulty understanding what is happening, anxiety about their medical conditions, or other reasons. And, metaphorically, comedians often do the same thing with their routines: marshal people into a state of relative comfort and ease – but at least they get a response to their funny, funny jokes.*

· · ·

I'm often apprehensive about the responsibility that comes with being a carer. Even now, after years of service, there'll be a moment during a shift when I step outside of myself and, glancing at this shrivelled person in front of me, am aware of how utterly helpless they are – and that all responsibility for them has been ceded to me, a man who once couldn't pay his phone bill because he'd rinsed his money on a tattoo of a dog with tits.

---

* If there's an audience member who's particularly stubborn and resistant, I turn them into my 'dad' and spend the rest of my set trying to make them proud of me. Hecklers, on the other hand, I sometimes pay to quieten down a bit. I once balled up a £20 note and paid it to a particularly drunk, aggressive woman at the Edinburgh Fringe. If anything, she became even more voluble – but still kept the £20.

My care work is in some ways a holdover from my teenage years working in a pet supply store. Except my wards then, of course, weren't human beings; they were hamsters, rabbits, chinchillas, love birds – even seahorses and Japanese fighting fish. *All living things are sacrosanct.*

This was my first foray into the world of work, and I was always self-conscious about the impression I was making and aware of the potential for misunderstandings; for confusion, antagonism, *embarrassment.* I remember one day, a customer returned a dog house and my colleague stored it in the manager's office for it to be processed. I gained entry to the office and crawled inside the house so I could scare my manager.* But when he reappeared he was accompanied by his own supervisor and the CEO, and their rendezvous promptly turned into a meeting about budgets. I'd left it too long to show myself. I waited for 45 minutes, bunched up with throbbing joints and breathing difficulties. Eventually it was too much. I poked my bum out and slowly crawled backwards while each of the men stared blankly at my unexpected emergence. 'I reckon that should be fine,' I said, standing up and rapping the top of the dog house with my knuckles – before nonchalantly walking out.

I also had a very brief 'thing' with a deputy manager. It was consensual. I never felt threatened or pressured into a sexual relationship. And it wasn't a traumatising experience for me. But revisiting it years later, knowing I was 17, a late bloomer, and she

---

* You've gotta get your jollies where you can!

was more than a decade older, there's something slightly uneven, slightly wonky, about the pairing. This was never acknowledged. No concerns were raised. She wouldn't have known how young I was in my head. But there was an implicit understanding that what was happening between us was a secret.

We'd go to her house, a place she shared with another one of our colleagues, and she'd lie down on the sofa, her head resting on my lap. There was a chasm between us: I was a teenager in trackie bottoms, a stubborn roll of puppy fat hanging on my midriff like a child's rubber ring, in a sexual relationship with an *adult* – a competent, financially stable adult (she drove us to restaurants and paid for our meals). She had a mortgage! And I had an acquaintance who made a video of himself fucking a Teletubby doll! And whenever we were in a restaurant (well, more often a biker bar on the edge of farmland intersected by pylons) I was self-conscious. I was worried onlookers would mistake her for my mum.

And there was another part of this story that affected me; there was a third person who played a peripheral role in this relationship. My manager's friend had a little boy, a toddler, with severe learning difficulties. I can't recall exactly what kind of learning difficulties he had. But sometimes my manager had to look after him while I was there.

I remember observing the toddler, his eyes adrift. He seemed vacant, passive. Unknowable. I had no way to access his inner stock of agency. At 17 years old, this shook me. This was a liaison that already seemed quite *heavy* – and now we were incorporating a vulnerable dependent. I was in college! And in college I was friendless. And now here I was, having to look after a kid – at least vicariously.

It was initially jarring. I'm ashamed to say it, but I struggled to see him as fully human because I wasn't equipped with any knowledge about his condition or an understanding of cognitive disabilities. But I tried to establish an affective dimension, to reach out and demonstrate care, concern and connection. And I did this by poking his nose like he was a doorbell. He winced, and paused – and then he started to cry.

'I don't think he liked that.'

My manager, meanwhile, was brilliant. She played games and spoke to him in a way that filled this little boy with vitality. I just didn't have the tools, or the experience, to do the same. We were chaste and responsible while looking after this kid – he was our primary responsibility. Still, if my first (proper) sexual experience was depicted in a fresco, in the corner there'd be a small, wary putto surveying a field full of bikers and pylons.

The inappropriateness of our relationship aside, I came away from it respecting the effortless way my manager bonded with this little boy, and treated him with love and affection – it showed an admirable moral weight to her character. An attentiveness and sensitivity. It's an ethical foundation that's missing in a lot of people, and I find it proper appealing. Also, in the upheaval of those teenage years, it was the first time I was a participant in the adult world of responsibility – especially being responsible for the welfare of another person. A *vulnerable* person. I'd briefly upgraded from looking after hamsters to – in some small way – looking after a human being. The entire situation made me feel out of my depth. (I'd have the same feeling during my first ever care shift.)

The way we deal with the burnout and the demoralising nature of work – especially the soulless, transactional nature of retail – isn't always rational. During my time at the pet store, I once had to assist someone with loading a hutch into their car. When I helped customers carry their items to their cars, I'd usually take my time walking the length of the business park, back to the mayhem of the shop. It gave me space to breathe, away from customer gripes or squawking parakeets or the rattle of the air conditioner.* But on this day, standing in the car park and watching the manic rush of weekend shoppers filter in and out of the entrance, I couldn't bear it. I couldn't go back inside. I couldn't have another conversation about how the EU was stopping a customer from breeding macaques in their flat in Tilbury. It was an existential herniation. The social self that enables me to be in a room full of other people – the presentable version of Pope that I bring to work – drained away. So I just silenced my

---

* In-store I'd find this sanctuary, this island of calm, either in the warehouse or sitting on an upturned tub of fish food in the narrow passage behind the tanks. Shrouded in the whir and glug of pumps and water. If customers focused their eyes while looking through the glass, beyond the fish, they'd see me sleeping.

phone and carried on walking until I arrived home. I bought a Magnum on the journey and hid in the garage until 9pm to avoid an interrogation from my mum. I had 42 missed calls.

On my next shift I was inevitably summoned to the manager's office. And in a bold but ill-thought-out bit of deception, I pretended I'd entered a fugue state on the previous shift and couldn't remember walking off. 'Now, this is proper weird and I know it sounds like I'm lying …'*

There have been a couple of shifts where I've walked away from the care home too. Where I've arrived at work, looked ahead and seen the mad rush that precedes breakfast – the washing, dressing and transporting to the dining room – play out in my mind's eye. In order to cope you have to take each minute as it comes, and be firmly rooted to the present, as a form of denial. You're denying the same strenuous, back-breaking routine that unfurls each morning, and getting through the isolated 'scene' you're currently in. It's an even more truncated version of the Alcoholics Anonymous adage 'One day at a time'. But if you envision the hectic morning in its totality – it can be too much to take.

One time when I was already feeling rough and had acute pain in my bowel (thanks to a mixture of Crohn's disease and opiate abuse), I got seven minutes into a shift, caught a whiff of shit that'd been left in one of the communal toilets by a resident, and waved my white flag. The olfactory assault forced

---

* I committed to it so completely that I was booked in for a CAT scan.

me to confront the reality – the unbearable reality – of what my job entailed. And if you're not focusing on the *right* stuff (the affectional ties, the intimacy and connection, the *helping* people) it's wall-to-wall shit.

I walked into the home manager's office, held up my hands and said, 'I'm really struggling and this has finished me off. I can't face it. I need to go home.'

She replied, 'You've been here less than ten minutes.'

Still, she let me leave. There had been a bit of a build-up beforehand, and an extended period of depression and suicidal ideation. But on that day, for whatever reason – whether it was a spontaneous psychic break or perpetual exhaustion – it was as if I'd escaped servitude. I hopped on a train to London and booked myself an overnight stay at a Premier Inn. In the evening I visited a bar where they practise Latin dance. I sat on my own, drank five white Russians and read a book about Fred and Rose West. Then I returned to the hotel room for some heavy slumber.

And, still, years later, I experience the same herniation. The same dread.

• • •

It's 8.15am. As I was late, I've been allocated the 'singles' (the people who only require the help of one care worker in the morning). I've already managed to assist three residents with washing, dressing, toileting, and so on. They're fairly mobile so the most time-consuming part of the job – fitting the sling and hoisting a resident, which requires two people – wasn't necessary. As I attend to them in their bedrooms I'll put on a podcast* or Radio 4 as a bit of background noise – with their permission, of course – just in case they're not in the mood for chatting, but usually they are.

Each room has an en suite so I'll fill the sink with warm water, put the disposable wipes in, and – if they're not already awake – gently rouse them by placing my hand on their shoulder. Depending on their mood I'll either be no-nonsense and practical (sitting them up, opening their wardrobe and presenting them with a selection of clothes to choose from) or playful (singing them an impromptu song to the tune of 'Sound and Vision' by David Bowie: 'Joan, Joan, Electric Joan / You like to speak on the phone', shit like that).

If we compartmentalise a 14-hour shift, it has four sections, and each of them is geared towards either mealtimes (breakfast, lunch and dinner) or bedtime. The morning rush, the current period, is the most laborious *and* the most time-constrained part of the day. Task-oriented behaviour, and rushing to complete a task within a given time frame, might be effective when you're working in manufacturing or distribution, but to apply what Simone Weil refers to as the 'icy pandemonium' of factory work to the care professions – it's a recipe for disaster. And it will always lead to institutionalisation, because it doesn't make room

---

* I once played an episode of *This American Life* that unexpectedly mentioned anal sex. Jane, whose hair I was brushing, exclaimed, 'Anal sex! It's far too early for any anal sex!'

for the mess of being a person. What if Electric Joan wants to try on another dress before going to the dining room? What if Jane wants to finish listening to the podcast about anal sex? It doesn't matter. We receive an implicit instruction to refuse to accommodate this – because residents *have* to be in the dining room, starting breakfast, at 9am. If they're not, it has a domino effect and sets us back for the rest of the day.*

I quickly return to the staffroom beside the reception. I reach for my rucksack, slung on top of the lockers, to retrieve my phone charger. I notice there's a new memo on the wall-length pinboard, divided into two columns: 'Things You Might Say to a Client†/Things You Should Say Instead'. The first example: 'Mrs Lady is mental/Mrs Lady has frontotemporal dementia'.

To be told how to speak is one of many little indignities at the hand of unwanted corporate paternalism that chips away at you. With this memo there's an insinuation, from those chair-swivelling dickheads in 'upper management', that we can't be trusted to have a conversation with another person without a script. And this standardisation of language is *another* stepping stone to institutionalisation; it erodes our affective abilities as we carers start to sound like automatons – which is how most of upper

---

* There was one CTM who'd whip the duvet off of a resident if they weren't ready to get out of bed yet, so I once poured a bucket of cold water over her and said, '*That's* what it feels like to them.'
† 'Client' is now the preferred term, but I stick with 'resident' (homely) or 'elder' (because of its connection to tribal culture).

management sound during site visits anyway, crouching in front of residents and talking to them with a patronising tilt of the head. I remember one of them once strode into our dining room wearing a three-piece suit and asked, 'Is everyone having a safe afternoon, ladies and gentlemen?'

I go to the fridge in the staffroom to retrieve my cans of Diet Coke. I'm sleep-deprived, so I'll probably get through about eight of these by the end of the shift. This is just one of the consequences of the high burnout rate for those working in the care sector – a sector where the bottom line is the driving priority.*

I'm in black shoes, black trousers and a black long-sleeved T-shirt rolled up to the elbows. Fundamentally I think most comedians are outsider, anti-establishment personalities – but petty rather than punk – who'll take any opportunity to assert their independence, even if it means faking a commitment to a Quaker mode of dress to avoid wearing a healthcare tunic, which is exactly what I do. An important touchstone of the Quaker faith is plain, unostentatious clothing – an outward custom to reflect our religious interiority – alongside a commitment to

---

* I often photocopy book extracts (re. social care) and hand them around to people in the care home, but – and I can't stress this enough – no one gives a flying fuck. I think it's because they're either not invested in this work (they just want to get their head down and get on with it) or they have more faith in their intuitive sense of 'good care' or they don't give a shit what the little college bitch boy is telling them to read.

egalitarianism and refusal to arbitrarily obey authorities. Whenever a regional director, or someone from head office, asks me why I'm not wearing a tunic, I cite the freedom of religion section of the Human Rights Act 1998.

'I don't want to be adorned with a corporate logo! I'm trying to be a good Quaker and reject the hierarchy of a corporate structure,' I said the last time this was questioned, having memorised the response from a note on my phone.

'What about the Real Madrid logo on your rucksack there?' asked the RD.

'Excuse me for a moment. I have diarrhoea,' I responded.

Upper management assume I'm being awkward or uncooperative for the sake of it. But this sort of defiance of the status quo is essential when it comes to pushing against the business-over-welfare model of profit extraction.

The fixation on profit has been disastrous for the care sector – and even the most trivial and petty acts of insubordination can have a positive impact on a work shift. I don't care what the company directors say. We *won't* be using peanut butter sparingly! I'll turn lights *on* when I'm leaving the room! I'll make sure I hit every corner when transporting food or medicine trolleys! I'll take up smoking just so I can do it near an oxygen tank!

Having said that – my main reason for not wearing the tunic is because it's tight around my love handles.

. . .

'I'd stick with the big pads and catheter lads. At least you've got some kind of protection. Ain't it, Pope?' says Tracy, a hyperactive fellow care assistant, elbowing me in the ribs.

Tracy has red hair pulled back into a messy bun. She also has a jutting jaw and bulbous eyes and wears a uniform that's several sizes too small so it cuts her torso into segments. Sometimes, in the winter when it's freezing, she gets rid of the uniform altogether and turns up in a knitted jumper that reads 'I'm bitch' ('I forgot the "a"!') – at least until a manager tells her off. She usually has a Vivienne Westwood pendant around her neck and her nails are generally painted various different shades of neon.

Within care home lore Tracy is famous for frantically searching for 'Arthur's socks' – despite Arthur having no legs. And despite Tracy knowing this because she'd been caring for him since he'd arrived in the home.

'Pat! I said if I had to share a bed with any of 'em I'd choose the big pads and catheter lads.'

It's now 11.15am and I'm in the care team manager's office. Breakfast has finished. It was tea and toast, with a choice of butter, peanut butter, jam or marmalade. This was followed by either porridge or cornflakes. And then everyone was offered a yogurt and fruit.

It usually takes about two hours to finish breakfast as transferring 22 residents from room to room (that's how many are in the unit I'm overseeing today) can be very demanding. Approximately a dozen of these need to be hoisted, three are bed-bound, and the remainder require a walking aid plus a carer to supervise them. Almost everyone needs help being taken to the toilet. Nine of them are assisted with their food. There are also catheters to empty, incontinence pads to change, arguments to break up, a few remaining beds to be made, family members to appease, a dining room to be cleaned and organised in preparation for lunchtime, dishes to be washed and dried (by hand), wounds to be redressed, drinks to be topped up, more teas to be made ... The list goes on and on. And there are only three carers. And a lot of people have been assessed for two carers, so if one of them needs to go to the toilet, that leaves one remaining carer – who is unable to leave the lounge, where the majority of the residents are sitting, in case one tries to stand up and takes a tumble. It's a constant game of Whac-A-Mole. Once all the loose ends have been tied up, *that's* when we can start the paperwork for 22 people.

The carer doing the fluid and nutrition paperwork – a record of what everyone has eaten and drunk, and the exact time they did it (and *none* of it is computerised) – remains in the lounge to keep an eye on everything there. I'm completing the daily observation charts. These files are covered by the Data Protection Act so they mustn't leave the CTM's office. I mark down the kind of personal care each resident has received and write a few paragraphs about their morning so far: their general demeanour, any aberrant behaviour, any interactions we've had with them, any concerns that were raised, etc. There are empty boxes of chocolate littering the top of the filing cabinets and a mini Christmas tree on Pat's desk. A drab bit of tinsel, liberated on one end, hangs listlessly from the pinboard.

'I'd pick Little Reeni, I reckon,' says Pat, giving it some genuine consideration, while leaning back in her desk chair. Her fingers are slotted together, resting on her barrel-like stomach. Pat also rejects the crimson tunics that are meant to be worn by CTMs. She has a beige one, issued to her over 15 years ago. She never let it go. 'Her room always smells lovely,' Pat continues. 'Her daughters make a fuss of her. Make sure it's kept nice in there.'

She then transitions into a low, conspiratorial whisper: 'And I know one of the husbands hates it because she cut their holiday short to look after Mum. But they're on it – without going full Louise. That's the way it should be, isn't it, Pope?'

I was reluctant to get involved, heavy with residual tiredness, but now I'm part of this.

'Yeah, probably June. Or Susan D. in room 19. She's completely compos mentis so she'll ask to go to the toilet. And I chat to her about visiting Winchester. Or what's happening with the Labour Party. I can have a proper laugh with her so, yeah …'

'Rather her than Billingsgate in room 5,' replies Tracy, an eager smile forming on her face and a light going on behind the eyes.

'Why Billingsgate?' I ask.

'Billingsgate Fish Market.'

There's a pause.

'Enough of that! No. No, I'm not 'avin that. We all like a laugh and joke …' shouts Pat.

Tracy, with a broad grin and wide eyes, poking my shoulder, hoping I'll be a willing accomplice, says, 'It's proper Billingsgate, isn't it, though. And don't blame me! I'm the one who has to deal with it! I'll have a pound of plaice but not from down there, thank you very much!'

'No. Nope. I'm not part of this,' I reply.

This is cruel, and demeaning, and I hate it. I'd never show any outward signs of encouragement – but there's something about how relentlessly inappropriate Tracy is that, in some circum-stances, despite that it knocks my moral compass off course, I get a flicker of enjoyment from. It's something akin to the pathetic genius of teenage boys, railing against politesse. And Tracy is fundamentally anti-social – rude, brash, histrionic, self-pitying. Awful to work with. But she has her moments.

Still – this isn't one of those occasions. And despite my usual permissiveness when it comes to joke-making, there's a point where it goes too far and irredeemably sullies the conversation.

I know that later in the day I'll spend an extra couple of minutes with the lady in room 5 as an act of contrition. (Similar to the 'compassionate clean-up' I'll do when Pat, or another carer, has been a bit brusque with a resident. Though Pat would never talk about a resident in such terms.) And when I see her, small and frail in an oversized chair, fastidiously reorganising the tissues on her side table, and looking up to give me an 'It's all in order' smile as I stand in the doorway, I'll hate Tracy. I'll hate Tracy for reducing this woman – a childhood spent in the Scottish Highlands; an accent refined by the elocution lessons of teacher training; holidays in Margate; a weekend in St Ives; all the snippets and fragments of personal history that build an incomplete biography of the person you're caring for – to a symptom. A symptom to be mocked. And how easy it is to do this when you're regularly presented with a tabulation of ailments or examples of faltering selfhood.

'So we gave her a dipstick and, as expected, she has a UTI. Let's keep pushing fluids,' says Pat. 'Room 6 can have a bath later this afternoon because he refused last week and the room, well ...'

'Stinks like shite!' shouts Tracy, unable to match the downtempo of this morning's congregation. As the morning shifts are notoriously hectic, we just want a moment to drink a coffee, or an energy drink, or a Diet Coke, without someone honking in our ear. The care home version of sitting behind the fish tanks. (Actually, because of the glass panel that looks out onto the corridor, when the door's closed, and passers-by have to rely on lip-reading to satiate their nosiness, the CTM's office is like the *inside* of the fish tank.)

'Pure shitey smell,' says Tracy, looking at each of us to see who'll make eye contact – teeming, thyroidal eyes that bulge forward and are invasive, like the rest of Tracy's nature. Her lack of spacial awareness and personal boundaries; her poking and tactility.

'My God, woman,' says Ligaya, who has also been sitting with us, exasperatedly pressing her fingers into her temples. Ligaya has a slight Filipino accent that could be mistaken for American, with thinning jet-black hair tied up at the back, a silk scarf and wingtip glasses. She's sitting upright with her knees pressed together. Like Pat she's in her sixties and also occupies a matri-archal role within the workforce – though she's a different kind of matriarch. Unintimidating but with an unexpected penchant for swearing. We talk a lot about international affairs and, even though she's tender and patient with the residents, she once told me she supported Duterte's extrajudicial killing of drug addicts. 'It's a real problem over there. And I wouldn't want you to die, but sometimes ... for the greater good, you know!'

'Yes! Shut your bloody mouth, will you, Tracy,' says Pat, 'or I'll staple the soddin' thing shut' – the last bit out of the side of her mouth.

'Ah, you all love it, really!' answers Tracy, once again elbowing me in the ribs, to a room full of people demonstrably not loving it. 'You don't know what you'd do without me and my mouth!'

'I'd stop having to take my blood pressure tablets for a start,' says Ligaya, to a ripple of laughter from Pat and me. Tracy is blank-faced. Sometimes when she's on the receiving end of it, a seriousness calcifies her usually elastic expression.

'Anyway – get on with your books,' says Pat. 'We're already behind as it is. And I don't want to get it in the neck because the rest of you are having a mothers' meeting.'

. . .

'He can have a right old chew on mine! No questions asked,' Tracy shouts down the corridor, halfway through a conversation with an inductee, hoping to drag other people into the fold.*

I think I heard someone mention Robert Pattinson. The girl is small and timid, lost in an oversized tunic. She laughs nervously. With the tip of her index finger she traces the raised purple scars going up her forearm. I already know this will be her final day.

When people begin working here they need to do two shifts shadowing another carer to get a sense of the workflow and the person-centred care and, the main reason, to shake them out of the assumption that their duties will be 'tea and sympathy' and nothing more.

The job's laborious; mentally taxing. And you don't get much in the way of compensation. Well, that's if you become too jaded

---

* I read a book by Sarah Perry where she summarises the Essex girl archetype – in a way that's supposed to be celebratory – as an 'irredeemably vulgar, plump, sexually threatening, feckless and indolent woman, an affront to morality, and a threat to the values of sobriety, industry and obedience that props up the ruling class'. She goes on to argue that there's something 'pleasingly anti-establishment about the Essex girl'; a 'woman who shrugs off the demands of respectability and a nicely guarded reputation'. There's a bit of Tracy in this.

or disillusioned. I stay in the job because it gives me a connection, and kinship, with residents, family members and other staff members – moments where, in the words of Peter Handke, in his 'Essay on Tiredness', it's like there are

> two people facing opposite ways, travelling opposite ways, revolving upon each other, [Person A] reaching forward with outstretched hand, [Person B] forward with outstretched hand, and neither able to move* till their hands have grasped each other, when they draw towards each other from opposite directions, draw nearer and nearer, each travelling in [their] separate cycle, till the two are abreast, and side by side, until even they pass on again, away from each other, travelling their opposite ways to the same infinite goal.

These tenuous moments keep me ticking over; provide uplift. But they're soon scuppered by Tracy, clomping along the corridor like a drunk goose, shouting, 'My tits! He can have a chew on my tits any day of the week.'

We begin lunch at about 12.45pm, so, having finished the daily observation books, I walk towards the lounge, giving myself half an hour to transfer everyone *back* to the dining room. As I'm passing, I look into an empty bedroom. There's dappled light

---

* Maybe due to the Parkinson's.

on the ground. Outside the window, afternoon traffic starts to build. And I notice the homeless guy standing motionless with his sleeping bag tied around his waist like a sweatshirt. He raises a can of beer to a passing jogger as a gesture of solidarity.

CHAPTER THREE

AT THE RATE HE'S GOING, SOON WE'RE GONNA BE DRIP FEEDING AN EAR ON A VELVET PILLOW.

DELICIOUS.

I
t's the day after the Christmas fete. I didn't attend because, even though I wasn't booked in for a shift, I would have been roped into doing care duties anyway. (Instead, I went to Canvey Island and shared a packet of crisps with a Hasidic Jew. Enough said.) According to Pat, everyone had a nice time. Some of the residents danced and shimmied; a few of them panicked as they realised they'd yet to buy presents. ('Don't worry! We've sorted it!' assured the carers.)

After morning handover* Pat whipped out her phone to show me a series of photos. It can be difficult to capture the fun the

---

* 'Dorothy ate some face cream last night.'

residents are having as old people aren't as demonstrative with their emotions. Most of the pictures were of Charlie Big Trousers, his red face beaming like brothel lighting as he 'twerked' in front of the residents, who passively observed the spectacle while propping their heads up with their hands.

Charlie Big Trousers is one of the entertainers who performs an afternoon show for the elders. There's a few of them on regular rotation: a lady with a bongo who sings about sausages in a high falsetto; a harpist; a male sitar player who passive-aggressively asks me about my 'writing' – then, apropos of nothing, boasts about singing to an old lady who's related to the surrogate mother of Elton John's baby.

Whenever I'm speaking or writing about elderly care, I try to avoid the sanitising effects of sentimentality. All it does is provide a palatable version of ageing that is both unhelpful and deeply irresponsible. And if that's the only thing that's being offered – a false account of care home life adopted to avoid corrupting someone's delicate sensibility – then people aren't accustomed to the realities of deterioration. The knock-on effect is this: when a member of the general public is presented with, say, coprophagia (the eating of faeces) or uncharacteristic libidinous behaviour from a relative who used to be a nun (yes, really – I'll leave the details to your imagination), it can be too confrontational, too much to take. And when people reach their experiential limit, they tend to look away, which leads to neglect or deprivation. I'll go as far as to say that I find twee and saccharine representations of care homes moderately unethical.

But there are times within the care home when the warmth of sentimentality *is* appropriate. If I can indulge the nice side of caregiving for one moment: I've found that anything with a musical component – especially wartime/post-war music – seems to ignite an inner reserve of joy within the residents. At such times, it's heartening to see a group of people, with bodies and minds that are now slack and failing, suddenly rediscover the elan of their youth.

Any meaningful activity – whether it's completing a household chore or a work-related task, or a recreational endeavour like having a sing-song or playing a game of catch – positively impacts a resident's well-being. They're still able to attain the sense of connection that derives from social involvement, so, regardless of their cognitive impairment or level of dependency, we make opportunities for them to participate in stuff that's purposeful.

According to Pat, when Charlie failed to capture his audience's attention by twerking, he tried a different approach. He invited a resident to join him 'onstage' – not realising Emma, the woman he chose, was very frail and unsteady on her feet (she became bed-bound not very long after this). In the next photo, Emma is rigid but almost vertical, and a carer in the background runs to her aid, while Charlie – a panicked look on his face, bunched-up rolls of fat under his chin due to the physical strain – is grabbing hold of her, attempting to catch her before she falls. Due to the way

Emma's body is positioned, with a look of complete indifference on her face, it's as if Charlie is about to use her as a battering ram.

'Look! Not a care in the world,' laughed Pat, talking me through what had happened.

'Why were you still taking photos?' I ask.

'So we could blame Charlie if she fell. He's a piss 'ead anyway.'

Charlie – who's about 50 years old – hasn't even got big trousers. That's the thing. They're chequered and tailored, with a 40-inch waist. He can't sing. Or dance. Or stand upright for longer than 15 minutes at a time. His entire act is wearing chequered trousers and a baker boy cap, and slurring his way through a medley of songs* – each one punctuated by a joke from *The Bumper Book of Horny Jokes*.

I think I overheard him telling one of the family members he'd never married. And one humid summer evening, I saw him down Southend seafront perched on the edge of a tidal wall. He was shirtless, revealing a big freckled back, tufts of ginger hair sprouting out of his shoulders, a distended belly and an angry-looking sunburn. He kept swigging from a bottle of Heineken and looking out at the horizon with the kind of cold, dead-eyed stare that signals impending violence. It took me a minute to notice the rasher of raw bacon attached to his handline, listlessly dancing in the water like a benzo'd belly dancer.

He was crabbing.

---

* During a rendition of 'LOVE' by Frank Sinatra, he spelt out the word 'LOAF' accidentally.

He was crabbing on his own.

He was knocking back Heineken while crabbing on his own.

I didn't approach him, or give him a nod of recognition, because the entire scene had the air of 'personal crisis'.

His 'stage' name makes no sense. And with each passing year the chequered trousers become tighter, meaning the name slips further into irrelevance.

He has a dog-eared copy of *The Bumper Book of Horny Jokes* intended for an audience who are unable, or unlikely, to have sex ever again.

And he's devoted a large portion of his life to entertaining that same audience, made up of people who forget he even exists, or that they're even part of an audience.

Maybe that's why he's knocking back beers while crabbing on his own.

• • •

It's 7.30am. After handover I walk to the lounge to retrieve the one functioning kettle and move it to the dining room. That way, once it's plugged in and the water has boiled, the tea is ready to pour.

In the dining room, I like to organise all the equipment we'll be using in advance of anyone's arrival so that when they're seated, they don't have to wait for a drink, a piece of fruit or a biscuit prior to the arrival of the food trolley. (This has heated compartments for either porridge or the pathetic morsels the home refers to as a 'cooked breakfast': one bit of bacon, one fried tomato, a spoonful of scrambled egg.) It's a bit of foresight that makes a world of difference in this line of work: by conveniently positioning the items, I create an unobstructed workflow. I can pour the tea, add sugar or sweetener, stir, put on their cloth apron and offer them a choice of orange juice, apple juice, blackcurrant squash, etc., without wasting time trying to find everything. Unlike in every other part of my life, in some ways I *thrive* in the care home. I'm efficient and organised. I can even multitask. I'm smashing it (at least some of the time).

After I fetch the kettle, and check that the medicine cupboard is locked (thus eliminating any temptation to sample the wares), I overhear Susan W. (*another* one of the Susans) calling out from her bed. She does this every morning when she's ready to get up – rather than press the buzzer connected to the central alarm system. I've been assigned the singles again today (my choice; I can't be bothered to talk to other carers first thing in the morning), so it makes sense to start with her.

She looks tanned and healthy. Her teeth are her own. And she still wears clothes for style as well as comfort. Some sequins, some lace, some off-the-shoulder numbers. A young-ish old. 'Marvellous for her age.'

She's married to Cliff, who, like his wife, is a healthy-looking 80-year-old. Tall and broad-shouldered. A former wrestler. And he, too, has a deep tan. I always imagine them as characters in a John Updike novel – having never read a single John Updike novel. But he's clearly devoted to his wife (I know there's a lot of adultery in Updike novels) and makes the effort to visit her every day after lunch.

She had a stroke a few years back that left her paralysed on one side of her body. Her right hand is permanently clenched – and so tightly that her fingernails are embedded in her palm. She was given a 'therapy carrot' (a carrot-shaped cushion that's inserted into the hand) to pry the fingers away from the palm and prevent puncturing. But carers often forget to put it in place. It's a small oversight but one with knock-on consequences. Dirty nails. Open sores. Initial discomfort leading to the pain of swollen fingers. And, finally, the smell that confirms infection. By that point, you're nothing but the smell. And Tracy – tactless, irresponsible Tracy – will hold her nose around you.

Despite her paralysis – and with the help of a walking frame, an accompanying carer and a lot of perseverance – Susan walks short distances. One foot forward, then she shifts her centre of gravity to swing the other foot in front. Chair to wheelchair. Across the bedroom to the toilet. She uses only her right thumb and the knuckle of her index finger to pinch the frame with her 'aggy hand' (as I refer to it). She's one of the few residents whose mobility has improved while she's been in the home.

Her dementia has made her paranoid. She's always worried Cliff's cheating on her. Or that he hasn't come to visit. Or assumes the other residents are conspiring against her. As a result, she cries a lot and throws around accusations. On one occasion, as I was assisting her onto the toilet, she responded curtly to my small talk.

'What's up, Susan?' I asked. 'What have I done to annoy you? And do you wanna give me a slap on the wrist?'

'Oh, you know what you've done,' she replied, turning her head away to break eye contact and make a point.

I was stumped.

'I really don't know what I've done! Let me know and I can try to rectify it.'

'It's as simple as that, is it?' she said, using her good hand to sprinkle fairy dust indiscriminately. 'And then things will magically go away.'

'Well, I can give it a go! What's happened? Have I been a herbert?' I asked, smiling, trying to defuse the situation. One of the many little acts of diplomacy you execute throughout a shift.

She banged her fist against the railing next to the toilet, like a stroppy toddler.

'I want you to have sex with me, Cliff! Is that too much to ask? I want you to *want* to have sex with me!'

I was shell-shocked.

'God, no! Susan, no! No, no, no. I'm not Cliff. I am *not* your husband,' I exclaimed. 'I'm Pope! I'm your carer! For the love of God – no!'

'You don't have to make up a whole new identity to get out of loving me, Cliff!' she shouted, her eyes beginning to water. (At that point, I had to call for a female carer to supervise. When I explained the situation, duly mortified, she found it very funny.)

But even though she has these delusional episodes, or misidentifies her reasons for being in the home, or her role within this environment, she retains plenty of day-to-day information: who the carers are (though that sometimes gets away from her), information about our lives, conversations we've had. And she recognises me (most of the time), and always says she's relieved when I'm on a shift, and refers back to *actual* anecdotes I've told her weeks prior to this. But still, there are other gaps in her knowledge: she usually knows me as 'Paul'. (I'm always correcting her on this but 'Pope' never sticks.) And in my spare time, I'm apparently restoring a nineteenth-century steam locomotive.

'How's the train coming along, Paul?' asks Susan.

She's in her adjustable bed. The top half is almost vertical, so she's sitting upright. Due to the metal plates and screws in her shoulder, this, according to her, is the most comfortable position.

'Getting there! Just mending the … tubes … of steam,' I reply, failing to summon any convincing railway terminology.

I lift up the side table next to the bed and move it to the corner of the room, beside the TV. I clear away some used tissues, mugs, magazines. The usual titivating to make the room presentable and clear a path for Susan to stumble to the toilet. You wouldn't expect it from a boy who has eaten painkillers he picked out of someone else's vomit, but I'm obsessive about tidiness and cleanliness. And I take pride in fulfilling a resident's preferences when it comes to the layout of their room. Or wanting things done a certain way.

'It's Laura's birthday today,' says Susan.

It isn't.

Laura is Susan and Cliff's daughter. She's in her late forties and has Down's syndrome. She shares a flat with her friend Naomi, who also has DS. They're part of a supported living scheme, so when she comes to visit her mum, Naomi and a nurse are usually in tow. Though sometimes she arrives with Cliff (who apologises for Laura's 'overfamiliarity' – but I always tell Cliff there's no need).

Whenever Laura sees me, she shows off her new football socks and asks for updates on her mum, or we roll our eyes at our respective jobs.

'It's been a bit hectic today but getting ahead of it,' I'll say.

'Gotta be done though,' she'll reply.

'Bringing home the bacon!'

'Yes. Bringing home for bacon.'

'I remember when I first had her,' Susan continues. 'It's not like it is now. Did you know the doctor urged me not to keep her?'

'Oof. It must have been proper hard back then, Susan. People didn't have all the information, did they,' I reply, stooping over the bed.

It's important to demonstrate engagement with a resident and stay close while you're talking, in case their hearing fails them. Especially if they're revealing something that's such a vital part of their personal history. Considering the heavy subject matter, I affect an almost pious bearing. But if the situation requires it, I can switch gears. I can gab! I can gossip! I actually had a subscription to *Heat* at one time. Sometimes Susan and I will look at 'scandalous' celebrity outfits, and she'll ask, 'Would your wife wear that?' (I haven't got a wife. I haven't got a train. What the fuck am I doing?) This is a good example of the social involvement that helps to improve a resident's well-being. It doesn't have to be elaborate. It can be as simple as flicking through a magazine. But this morning, for whatever reason, Susan wants to confide in me.

My role as an active listener, and an informal, unqualified therapist, is another important – and underappreciated – aspect of care work. Even if the money and the resources were there, these elders would never be referred for counselling or therapy by their GP. (The GP – who's also overstretched and under pressure – barely has time to look at swollen legs or infected sores, let alone the holistic side of things.) So who's able to fulfil this requirement? Who can attend to their psychological needs? That's us as well. And we're clearly not trained for this kind of responsibility. Any knowledge I've acquired has been through extracurricular study.

I do what's expected: I express uncomplicated sympathy for Susan's earlier plight. And I'm genuinely moved by her recollections. The intolerance she faced, the cruelty.

In elderly care you're not trying to encourage personal growth or train the residents for social acceptance like you would if you were caring for a younger person with a developmental disability.

There's a passage in Eva Feder Kittay's *Love's Labor: Essays on Women, Equality and Dependency* where she writes about managing one's expectations when caring for the elderly, and the caregiver's aim of tarrying the old person's demise: 'Care for the elderly requires fostering relevant self-sufficiency and self-esteem rather than fostering growth. Rather than socializing for acceptance, care for the elderly requires stemming a disintegration of that social acceptability* and sense of self-esteem which the individual attained while a vigorous adult.'

But even if we're hoping for different outcomes through our dependency work, I'm just as concerned about the depersonalisation or institutionalisation of my residents as is a care worker who oversees the welfare of those who are younger and have learning difficulties. And that's why I'll *always* encourage the full expression of their identity – their traits, their personal concerns – even if (as with Susan's tears and paranoia) it can sometimes be a bit of an imposition.

● ● ●

---

* I'd actually argue that the burden of change is on the 'right' side of society – or, in other words, that we should try to instil a more tolerant attitude when confronted with aberrant behaviour by educating people about the effects of neurodegenerative diseases or other mental disorders.

A few weeks ago, while standing in the care home's lounge, and switching over to a nature documentary on the TV, I had a conversation with Tracy about the 'mental qualities of a worm'.*

'Ooo, that's a funny-looking boy,' said Barry, noticing the worm onscreen.

I spoke about the worm's cerebral ganglia, the bundle of nerve cells in its head that acts as a substitute brain, and then Tracy – with other family members sitting and listening – made an unfortunate comparison between a worm and a severely disabled baby. Between a worm and a human being.

'It's the same, though,' she insisted.

'But it's not – and I don't think you can say that,' I replied.

'I don't think it matters. They don't even have ears, do they?'

(They do have ears.)

A couple of days later, after mentioning this interaction I had with Tracy, Mum and I started chatting about abortion, legal personhood and her experiences as an auxiliary nurse working the VTOP (vaginal termination of pregnancy) list.

'One of the doctors told me something that still haunts me,' Mum said.

It was 5am; pre-dawn and sepulchral. Alan (the dog) had woken her up to go for a slash, so she was in the lounge watching

---

* 'If worms are able to judge ... having drawn an object close to the mouths of their burrows, how best to drag it in, they must acquire some notion of its general shape'. This is from an essay by Oliver Sacks called 'The Mental Life of Plants and Worms, Among Others'.

The Real Housewives of Orange County. The only light source was the TV. And I was awake because after years of getting up at 5am to travel to work, or commute from Rayleigh to Portsmouth at university, I've been conditioned to wake up early, even if it isn't a work day. (This was on a day off.)

She was in a dressing gown, with her feet tucked underneath her bottom, emptying her daily supply of medication onto her lap. Blood pressure, fibromyalgia, asthma, depression, stomach ulcer. And still I assume she's indestructible, that she'll last forever!*

This is another one of those private salons.

The anchoritic safety of our lounge.

Conversing in our own private language, using our shared stock of references, just before the noise of the A127 migrates from down the road.

'She said it had a foot, a barely formed foot, and each time the vacuum approached, it pulled the foot up to its body.'

I shuddered. 'Jesus. That's fucking haunting.'

When you hear a detail like that, it hits you.

'Yeah, I wish she hadn't told me that. But she said it might have been a – what's it called? Like in the Robbie Williams one where they're all waking up?'

---

* There used to be opioid painkillers in the mix but, after years of me stealing them – finding the most obscure hiding places, behind every framed picture, in every coat pocket, buried inside coffee granules – she keeps them locked in a safe upstairs. I've often considered throwing it out of the window, onto the decking, hoping it'll burst on impact.

'*Awakenings*?' I answered, resisting the urge to correct 'Robbie'.

'Yeah. Might have been a ...'

'Reflex?'

'Yes! It might have been that.'

'If I had a baby like that,' she continued, 'and I knew someone was saying derogatory things, I'd be absolutely devastated.'

'Because you think it's too cruel?'

'I don't like it when people talk about what other people look like. People are lovely in their own right.'

'Even if they've got no brain? And people compare them to a worm?'

There's a theory that the punchline of a 'dead baby joke' (or any kind of transgressive humour) isn't the dead baby. It's the sanctimonious, pearl-clutching audience – people who tend to sentimentalise mental deficiencies – we imagine to be outraged by the joke. This was at the root of the exchange between my mum and me. Part of me wanted to pay penance for being disrespectful, for mugging off a baby. The other part wanted to elicit Mum's disapproval to make myself laugh.*

We've both worked in the medical profession, or had a job that's medically adjacent, so our tolerance for gallows humour is higher than that of someone on the 'outside'. We've seen the worst. We're used to it.

---

* For me, the main source of laughter is the absurdity of mugging off a tiny, innocent baby. Only a tiny, petulant man would pick such an undeserving target.

And if one of comedy's main aims is to show human weaknesses and limitations – well, this is one of my weaknesses: I have an occasional urge to submit to such cruelty under the guise of a joke.*

But as well as being desensitised to some pitch-black comedy, working in care has also forced me to make calculations about the potential harm of a joke or a throwaway remark – and to restrain myself when necessary.

If my instinct is to take the piss or position myself as the 'mortal enemy of sentimentality' – like Gaston Modot in *L'Age d'Or* cuffing an old lady or mistreating a blind man – then this is neutralised by a deeper understanding of the people I'm caring for and exposure to the repercussions of a joke. You're no longer an uncomprehending stranger depriving people of interiority. There's a person behind it. And is it worth ruining someone's day?

Most of the residents are people who can't adequately defend themselves, and attending to this kind of vulnerability, and dependence, makes the human cost of 'punching down' more stark. So I'm grateful to care work for supplying me with both moral discernment *and* an uncompromising comic sensibility.†

Carers *will* trade jokes about residents – jokes that outside of the privacy of an office or a staffroom would be perceived

---

* In private. And in this book.
† Shit. I'm gonna become one of those comedians who put duct tape over their mouths for promo pictures or call their hour special 'Truth Serum'. Embarrassing.

as tasteless – but we do it to alleviate the pressures of work and the surfeit of nervous energy. A spontaneous rebellion against social strictures. As comedian Ari Shaffir said to me when I told him about my suicide attempt, which I'd turned into material a week after the fact, 'You're a comedian. What else are you going to do with it?'

As carers, we bear witness to the later stages of life, so we partake in this kind of chat to counterbalance the tragedy of ageing. The slow but inexorable crawl towards an end where we're erased by flames as the curtain closes on our families. And from which point on we're forever behind the shroud. Separate. Separated.

Oof.

That's bleak as shit.

So the incongruity, the shift from solemn to silly sausage, is part of a healthy balance of propriety and impropriety.

In this spirit, when Arthur in room 25 had his second leg amputated, I said to the assembled workers, 'At the rate he's going, soon we're gonna be drip-feeding an ear on a velvet pillow. At least it won't shit as much.'

Still, even though I'll always opt for a *burst of laughter* over *moderate pleasure* (I'm a drug addict!), I'm not free of guilt when I submit to Cheap 'n' Nasty Pope. I know it's wrong. And I should probably rein it in a bit.* But there's always a complicated

---

* When my nan died, I told my mum I was going to use her corpse as a toboggan.

negotiation between freedom of speech and social responsibility, between liberty and decency.

* * *

I collapse the adjustable barrier attached to the side of Susan's bed. She often forgets she has problems with her mobility and, being an independently minded person, and one who raised a family with its share of adversity, she often tries to climb *over* this barrier, not fully accepting she's putting herself at risk – even after it's been explained to her.

'This stupid thing,' she says, dismissively waving her hand at the barrier. 'They try to keep me in bed but I just climb over it.'

'But then we find you tangled up in it, Susan!' I remind her. 'And if I'm taking you to breakfast, I don't want to have to take the barrier with me as well!'

We both laugh. This is the gentle, mild-mannered repartee I'll engage in with the residents so as not to rock the boat. Work Pope. Care Ethicist Pope. Sometimes it'll be a bit more risqué. And in such moments, when you forget yourself and go quite blue, and you're still met with raucous, delinquent laughter from the elders – that can be very rewarding.

On such occasions we have to remind upper management that we're all *adults* and we're capable of gauging who won't be fazed by adult themes. I'm not going to seek permission from them or family members. Consent comes from the people I'm making laugh. Now, Susan is one of those people. She doesn't mind a bit of rude. But this morning isn't the right time for it.

She leans forward and I put my left hand between her shoulder blades while she holds on to my right. I help to sit her up and bring her around so she's on the edge of the bed.

'It was a hard, hard time,' she says in a plaintive tone.

'Laura is doing so well now, isn't she. She's working, she's got her own place. She seems like a real comfort to Naomi as well. Like, their carer was saying Naomi needs a bit more help but Laura is putting on music and watching the footie and …'

'I don't think Laura understands. I think she's happy in her own bubble, but I don't think she understands.'

'What doesn't she understand, Susan?'

'That your train isn't going to be ready. Or that the steam pipes aren't going to be train,' she replies, looking at me with deep concern. And then, on the edge of tears, in a strained whisper: 'That the steam pipes aren't going to be train.'

As is common within the care home, the conversation momentarily falls apart.

I've read a pile of books about the idea of personhood or selfhood – and how we're bound to our social nexus and defined by our relation to other people. In one of them John Dewey proposed that 'the self has no meaning except as contrasted with other personas' and, as a consequence, 'the self and the world are correlative, and have the same content'.

This relational interactivity – the idea that the origins and foundations of the self emerge in reference to others – is a key part of social approaches to care. With any relationship, there's a fluidity to interaction – both to the other entities and the world at large. So carers have to be socially agile and adaptable, rather than forcing a resident into certain modes of communication. I've found it to be highly effective to open up space for people with dementia to participate in self-directed action, including the 'direction of travel' for our chit-chat. If Susan wants to talk about trains, then – *toot toot* – we're talking trains!

And because of my preference for the relational, social constructionist angle, I don't subscribe to a one-size-fits-all, essentialist view of dementia* – even if upper management promotes this by issuing notices on how to communicate with residents, implying they're a single homogenous unit. The most sought-after carers – the ones who residents and family members are pleased to see on shift, the ones people confide in or air their grievances to – are those who are adaptive and recognise the dynamic interplay that takes place within a social context (like me).

As Jill Manthorpe acknowledges in 'Decisions, Decisions … Linking Personalization to Person-Centred Care', support should be 'individualized or closely tailored, responsive and flexible'.

---

* This actually speaks to a larger issue I have with the erasure of 'self' – or its reduction to a neuronal Mexican wave – by those self-appointed gatekeepers of knowledge on the human brain: neuroscientists. Marilynne Robinson, in her essay 'Humanism', can articulate this argument better than I ever could: '[T]here could be no more naïve anthropocentricity than is reflected in the certainty and insistence that what we can know about the nature of things at this moment makes us capable of definitive judgements about much of anything'.

So, I make the immediate decision to keep our conversation flowing. I've often spoken to Susan about my depression, my job dissatisfaction, or arguments I had with my ex-girlfriend. (Like when I didn't notice our bedroom had flooded because I was too busy making a stop-motion animation of a sweetcorn wrestling a peanut.) She responds to this. And because of my willingness to treat her like a confidante, and the self-reinforcing bond of trust that is forged between two people exchanging information about their private lives, she regularly talks about past heartbreak and current anxiety. As carers, we can be inadvertently designated the role of secular priests or guardians of confession, along with all of our other functions: therapist, waiter, personal assistant, hair-dresser, strength and conditioning coach, and so on. We're Swiss Army support workers.

I'm a fan of chatting anyway – and *especially* when it's a deep, therapeutic conversation. I like the satisfying synergy that occurs when two people are igniting something in each other.

I love the practice of confession. The unburdening of inveterate confessors. It's been a big part of my life – as spiritual practice, as creative outlet, and as a method of forging trust between me and the person I'm caring for. It reveals the essence of a private, and scarred, humanity, which really helps to solidify a bond between two people.

Another aspect of conversation I like: when the free improvisation of a discussion momentarily finds its coherence – we're bonding! We're riffing! – before the judder of an awkward goodbye. As a comedian, you're always aiming for that sweet spot. And for this, I'm glad to be part of a world full of relational beings.*

A lot of drug addicts recognise that part of the reason they abuse substances is to restore a sense of connection with other people – but by using, and the anti-social lifestyle that comes with it, the sense of termination between the user and wider society becomes more entrenched. (This is further compounded by a pandemic.) Whether the dislocation is self-enforced, or whether it has social roots, you end up creeping around the edges of the day, only emerging to procure more pills, more tar or more powder – whatever it takes to combat a boredom that's rooted in a fundamental discomfort with who you are.

One of the books that helped me to understand my addictive nature was Gabor Maté's *In the Realm of Hungry Ghosts: Close Encounters with Addiction*. He believes that 'we despise, ostracize and punish the addict because we don't wish to see how much we resemble him. In his dark mirror our own features are unmistakable. We shudder at the recognition. This mirror is not for us, we say to the addict. You are different, and you don't belong with us'.

---

* I once did a work-in-progress show at Hot Water Comedy Club that turned into a semi-intervention. The only people in the audience were eight drunken aunties and one sweet, timid man. After abandoning my prepared material, I remained seated on the stool, under a spotlight, while all the aunties expressed genuine concern for my welfare and dispensed life advice. Once the 'show' had finished, they cuddled me as I was leaving. It was wonderful.

The old and the infirm are another reminder of our mortality, or the continuous thread that runs throughout our lives – our personhood – but the parts of it that are fraying, that are weakened, and could break at any moment. That's why they've been shunted into care homes eroded by the economic forces totally outside the control of those most integrally involved, whether as residents or carers. And why would you want to integrate these people when they're such a stark reminder of our fallibility? This is my main reason for feeling so comfortable kicking back with the Dementias. There might be differences in our subjectivity, or our capacity for rational thought, but we're all sidelined; we're all considered a burden. And what should outlaws, pariahs and desperados do when they find each other? Band together and start a gang.*

. . .

In 2016, when I was in the midst of active addiction, and Trump's prodigious ascent to the top of the Republican ticket (and finally the presidency) seemed unstoppable, I was at my lowest ebb. I was buried alive in a troubled relationship and, in between 14-hour care home shifts and heavy drug use (which consisted of half a bottle of 10 mg/1 ml oxycodone oral solution; an entire bottle of 10 mg/5 ml Oramorph†; 60 x 30 mg dihydrocodeine tablets

---

* Our insignia is two syringes crossing each other: one full of heroin, the other full of Ovaltine.

† I'd down this like a pint of Carling.

taken in one go), I obsessively catalogued the then-current events: Trump's history-warping narcissism, the kamikaze mission we called Brexit, the failed Turkish coup d'état, the rise of Rodrigo Duterte, et cetera.

Outside of work, and my mum, dad and girlfriend, my social life had completely evaporated. I wasn't even seeing my three closest friends, who I've known since I was two years old. And if we understand that individuals can extract meaning from their lives by existing within a network of relationships, a matrix of dependency, my boring ol' life was intersecting with very few other people's at this point. The people I *was* engaging with – those who ended up being a regular fixture within a given week – took on an outsized role in my personal narrative. And these weren't intimates. I didn't even know their names. But they entered, stage left, and they had an impact. I was starting to understand what this must be like for the elders.

Tom Kitwood – one of the most influential writers on dementia, particularly in the field of person-centred care – had ideas about personhood that didn't necessarily derive from abstract philosophical analysis, for he was always striving for an understanding that had real-world application. He felt that 'personhood lies at the meeting point between three discourses: transcendence, ethics and social psychology'. And, focusing in on the latter, with personhood being defined as a process grounded in social interaction, our assigned roles aren't always fixed, determinate categories.

So the inconsistency, and dynamism, that can take place during interactions between two or more people also applies to how we position ourselves in social arrangements or – going even further – how we think of our own identity.

My period of active addiction went on for about five years, but the worst of it was between 2015 and 2017. Back then I also did three 14-hour shifts per week, so I had the remainder of the week off. With my girlfriend working a typical 9 to 5, there was a lot of time spent on my own, sitting in a tiny room above a night-club and next door to a drug dealer. Our flat was nicely furnished; she'd turned it into the best possible version of itself. But being one of those tiny places above the high street, with a view of a broken street lamp and a betting shop, it had that atmosphere you couldn't enliven – despite coiling fairy lights around everything.

There was a woman who worked in a newsagent just around the corner from the flat, three doors down from the local police station, who sold me vodka. Going there was the only time I left the flat (other than to go to work). The shop was next to a larger convenience store with cheaper vodka, but I couldn't do it to her; it had the flavour of betrayal. I'd come in at the same time every day, in jogging bottoms and an Aphex Twin T-shirt. Before I'd even spoken she'd say, 'Morning, love,' reach behind her and plonk a 35 cl bottle of Glen's onto the countertop. (I always convinced myself that would be enough. I always went back for more – but at the cheaper convenience store, which stayed open later, so she would never know.)

She'd shoot me a knowing smile, a conspiratorial nod of the head. I interpreted the gesture as *'There's no shame in being a piss 'ead, piss 'ead. Just be careful. Keep your nose clean. Stay out of trouble. And no matter what happens, I'll always be here for you. Hand on the tiller. Guiding you to safer waters. Also, I love you and always will.'* Which was probably me projecting. But, for some reason, even though she was enabling me for profit, I was comforted by her. Much like I am to the residents, she was a constant, steady presence. A guardian – but one who happened to facilitate my alcoholism.

I've picked up a few of these over the years. They come into my orbit. But in some instances the roles have been reversed and *they're* the ones looking for love, or friendship, or simply someone to talk to. Like the man on the number 3 bus I'd travel home from work with if I was doing an early Friday shift.

Before he introduced himself to me I'd seen him initiate conversations with fellow passengers – they were always reluctant to participate, knowing they'd be trapped in this interaction. He was about 70 years old, with a bulbous nose, the tip of which had a constellation of burst capillaries. Raw-boned and skinny and nearly bald.* He hiked almost everywhere – traversing the fields of Rawreth, Essex,† like a nomad – and taught people how

---

* He once told me he gelled up the remaining hairs so they functioned as 'ant antennas' and stopped him from bumping his head.
† The biker bar I'd frequent with the deputy manager from the pet supply store was on the edge of one of these fields.

to use farming equipment. There was a salt 'n' soil quality to him. And he always had a plastic bag full of charity shop purchases – cassettes of people singing Tudor ballads, engineering books, assorted bric-a-brac – which would sway in time with the bus and clatter against his knees. As an unofficial custodian of local history, he provided a gentle, soothing boredom, which was nice after a manic shift. I thought of him as a lavender man.

Much like with the residents, I'd built up a half-formed impression of the man from a slow accretion of biographical details – from snippets he'd tell me during the bus ride. As it was on the Friday, he was travelling back from a church concert. And he'd complain that 'the contralto was reedy' or provide a detailed account of why he'd switched to egg mayonnaise sandwiches. He studied engineering at the University of Manchester. And in his early twenties he became the sole carer of poorly parents – which continued for most of his life.

But on one occasion, he boarded the bus with another man, and they both sat in the two remaining seats at the back of the bus next to me. (It was *always* rammed with day-tripping elders. And sometimes I just wanted to read so I'd duck down, hoping he wouldn't see me.)

We were in a line. I was sitting to his right. The new man was on his left. He was short and dishevelled. Stale. Wearing two raincoats, both with broken zippers. He had erratic, Žižekian hair; thin and greasy. And as he commenced a droning, relentless sermon – out-boring Lavender Man (who actually smelled like biscuits or the pads on a dog's feet) – LM turned to me, rolled his eyes and quietly muttered, 'He's always like this. Met him on the bus one day and I've never been able to get rid of him.'

• • •

Susan is sitting on the edge of the bed, wearing only pyjama bottoms.

'Can you lift up your arms and raise the roof for me, please, Susan? I need to scrub those pits,' I say, trying to defuse the potential awkwardness of a young man seeing an old woman in a state of undress.

Susan laughs.

'I can't lift them as high as I used to be able to,' she replies, feigning embarrassment.

As with any situation where someone's vulnerable and exposed, and the transfer of power can be exploited in the most malign and reprehensible ways, I reassure her by providing a running commentary of my actions or soliciting consent for each subsequent step.

'We'll scrub under the arms and then move onto the back if that's alright, Susan?'

This idea of rolling, ongoing consent – removed from its sexual context – means Susan retains both her personal autonomy and the ability to say no, and because of this she feels in control of the interaction and able to demarcate her own boundaries.

Though in this instance Susan knows me well enough to feel at ease in my company, to hold on to a sense of security.

She'll talk about the rubbish bras Cliff recently bought her – with straps that cut into her back – or tell stories about the trouble they had conceiving Laura. (*She* might be alright but *I'm* not always free of discomfort.)

Equally, I'm aware there's a foundation of trust between us, so I'm not restrained by formality when it comes to the type of conversations I initiate. The day before, she shared an anecdote about her school days, about a group of nasty bullies that tormented a younger girl.

'Remember yesterday, when we were chatting about those bullies?' I ask, drying her face with a towel.

'Yes! Yes,' she replies, as I drape the towel over the bed frame and spray deodorant under her armpits. 'Those girls from my school. There can be such cruelty in the world, can't there.'

I assist her with her bra (not one of the ones Cliff got her) by guiding her arms through the loops and doing up the clasp at the back. With her 'good' hand, she adjusts it in the front by tugging it down and then stuffing everything into the cups.

I show her a long-sleeved T-shirt that was on the back of her chair. She gives it a nod of approval. From the outside, I push my hand through the sleeve, hold on to her 'aggy' hand and roll the sleeve over her arm – and then she's able to slip the rest of it on. (It's such a simple method but one that often isn't used. I share it with new recruits as if it's a bit of ancient wisdom. Some of the carers end up trying to force her paralysed arm into the sleeve. And when she cries, they accuse her of being 'melodramatic'.)

'Good job you're a lovely young man,' she says, smiling.

'I had a naughty stretch, though, Susan! I was a bit of an arse-hole when I was in senior school,' I reply.

'I don't believe that for a second, Paul.'

'Honestly. When I was about thirteen years old. I split off from my best mate, Louie. We've been friends since we were babies. Still are. But when I was in year eight I briefly chased popularity like an idiot. Do you ever think about periods in your life as a sort of inflection point? That was one of mine.'

The group I temporarily became a part of was mix-gendered (when puberty calls!) and fraught with secret machinations.

There was low-level criminality too: stealing stuff (a tray of Kinder eggs from Woolworths and a TV from Comet – the police who visited my house arrived while I was watching a Celine Dion documentary on VH1); underage drinking; throwing a bag of human faeces at a passing car* and getting chased through the council estates by a man with a machete.

But at 13 years of age, knocking about with a group of boys who were prone to destructive boredom, things would tip over the edge. And when they did, I'd experience psychic tumult, but I was too pathetic to intervene – or intervene in a way that'd have any impact.

There was a woman we called Old Lady Agnes. She had nutty hair, a clumsy jaw and a face streaked with deep recesses,

---

* Mum. If you're reading this. It was Nathan. Nathan threw the shit. The one who stole money from Dad.

as if she were a lino print. She was always bundled up in an ankle-length puffer coat and walked around town, soliloquising incessantly but occasionally stopping to answer the voices that *weren't* inside her head.

We'd walk or ride beside her, not to harass but to genuinely extract some form of conversation. We sensed no one really took the time to get to know her, so we'd pepper her with questions. And she'd answer! And she was smiling, and calling us 'dear, lovely boys', so we had a real desire to bond. I never sensed that she was frightened or disorientated by our presence. Sometimes it was as if she were oblivious to the fact she had company.

Occasionally one of the boys would slip in a rude question to gauge her response.

'Oooo, I don't know anything about those kinds of things or what you're asking me there, boys, but I'll be sure to tell him to look it up because he knows more about these things than I do but that's the way it is and that's the way it wants to be ...'

The others would say it was harmless, but a creeping unpleasantness started to darken the walks we'd have with Agnes. They no longer seemed innocuous.

But, still, we let it pass.

It started with a few rude questions and us goading each other to push it that little bit further; but then this incremental process of testing and probing, as if this poor woman were part of a clinical experiment, led to one of the boys putting cooked chicken in her hood, another one sloshing drink onto her coat, and – the final nail in the coffin – someone spitting on her.

In this scenario, I was one of the 'good men' doing nothing so that 'evil' could triumph.

Evil is a stretch. We were stupid kids – really stupid kids – engaging in a bit of adolescent one-upmanship. And, unfortunately, this soured our (initially) benevolent intention to let an old, demented lady know she was part of society and wasn't being ignored.

But the thought of her walking along, spit on her back, while we sniggered in her slipstream – it still haunts me. Even then, it rattled my conscience. I'm sure it did the same for some of the other boys, but I couldn't get behind the senseless cruelty. I made a decision to part ways with the group and return to my childhood friend.

I tell Susan an abridged version. But it's the first time I've thought about Agnes in years, and, as I'm recounting this spate of adolescent callousness, I'm jarred by an unexpected rush of emotion. My eyes start to water.

I wonder if – deep down – care work is my form of penance. Or if I was always equipped with the emotional capacity needed for care work, but with Agnes I was working against my better nature. Most likely, both these sides co-exist within me and – much like everyone else – I'm forever working towards a form of homeostasis, trying to find some balance in the cost-benefit analysis of my own morality.

As a care worker I implement another type of cost-benefit analysis: negotiating between a person's right to self-determination and what's in this person's best interest. Do I stand back and allow a resident to exhibit the full spectrum of their personhood? Or do I intervene and stop them eating shampoo? But whether carers, managers and family members are trying to protect the resident, unburden themselves of the resident's 'demands' or fulfil time-oriented objectives, discussions around decision-making – especially the resident's capability to make their *own* decisions – aren't always prioritised. If we consider ourselves to be complex, multifaceted human beings, then we should see those who are living with dementia in the same light.

'I'm so sorry to hear about your dead brother,' says Susan, with soft eyes and a furrowed brow. 'And to think – you were *this* close to finishing your train. Anyway, I must go for a tinkle.'

CHAPTER FOUR
SHOULDERS BACK, MY DARLING! SHOULDERS BACK!

Today is Boxing Day. It's fallen on a Wednesday this year. But like a Sunday shift, there's no management, only CTMs. There'll be a slightly more relaxed, congenial atmosphere. Both staff and residents will be happier, and more patient with one another, so I won't be compelled to whip the heads off the daffodils that grow next to the car park. This also confirms how pointless and counterproductive it is for management to apply downward pressure. It's one of those tactics designed to assert status, extract labour. We already know what the job entails. What's the point in having it reiterated?

On the days when they're actually on shift, the home manager and deputy manager are in the main office (with the HM seated behind a desk in the middle and the DM perched on the edge, like a child in a sidecar), reading memos from upper management or company directors who, in turn, are working from the HQ near my house.* They're insulated. And, as a result, don't have a feel for the toil on the 'floor', no matter how often they remind you that they, too, were once lowly carers.

I follow Sarah Jaffe, an American labour journalist, on Twitter. To me, she's usually bang on when it comes to the plight of the modern worker – especially those who are part of the precariat. On the subject of intimate labour (or domestic labour or care work), she writes that it 'brushes up against the line between what we think should be done for love and what we think should be done for money'. I find that the further the members of upper management move up the ladder,† the more they lose their grasp

———————

* On my days off, I walk past the company HQ during my morning walk/jog/walk/have a donut. Recently I stopped and stared through the window at one of the senior team members as he sat at his desk, looking fretful during a phone conversation, tapping a pen on the ridge of his nose to release some of the percolating stress. To see him in this blank, Tupperware office – inadvertently exhibiting himself in this unguarded posture – it helped to humanise the 'enemy'. (Up to that point, I'd often considered flashing my arsehole to the senior team members and opening it up, as if tearing through a bin bag.)

† Where are all these competitors trying to get to? What's at the top of the ladder? I could say the motion towards attainment – the hours of hustling and networking, trying to build a career – is the ultimate province of meaning. But I learnt more about the nature of things from a low-paid, dead-end job; from picking up an 'omelette' of coagulated blood that seeped from the head of an injured old lady. (The main lesson there was some people have podgy blood.)

on what care work really entails, on the affectional ties between a resident and their caregiver.

As Jaffe puts it, there's a 'coercion behind the mask of love'. Intimate labourers are emotionally manipulated into committing to such work despite the 'privatization of stress, the proliferation of depression, and a rise in anxiety'. We carers and our overseers are split into these 'separate spheres' – profit being the driving motivation behind the shrewd, muggy upper managers' exploitation of the Sisyphean drudgery of their workers – so it's difficult for us, on our side of the fence, to see the benefits of shoving a new resident into a room that's barely been vacated by the last occupant.*

It's 2.40pm. Again, I'm late for work, but I'm only doing an afternoon shift. I was a last-minute replacement for a carer who rang in sick – probably to steal a few hours with their family over the holiday.

As I walk into the reception area I cast my eye over the wall of framed pictures behind the front desk. It's a grid made up of 8-by-12-inch photos, one for every staff member, with each person's name below. Due to the high turnover, frames are periodically removed or replaced. Some photos disappear; some appear; and – depressingly – some *re*-appear after a brief, though fruitless, hiatus. The picture of me is an old one. I'm grey-green

---

* When this happens, you can still smell the urine infection of the person who used to live there. You get a bit misty-eyed thinking about their infected piss.

with cavernous eyes. Emaciated. My hair's tied into a thick plait – emphasising my receding hairline. I look like a skull that's been vacuum-sealed using my own face as packaging.

As always, I'm working on the ground floor. I give Simon, in room 2, a quick wave as I walk past. (He doesn't see me. He's too busy steadying a miniature bottle of Jameson as he pours it into his coffee. If you catch him in the morning, you'll find him pouring it onto his cornflakes.*)

Edgar occupies room 31, in Symphony. He's retained some of his youthful dapperness, some of his whisky-tumbler charm. He reminds me a lot of a man I looked after in another home previously, who once escaped and managed to get to the pub over the road. This other guy was more rough-hewn than the slick, twinkly person you saw in his old photographs, but because there was enough of that remaining, and enough lucidity, he was able to pass as an independent old boy. The pub was full of people having their Christmas work do. He successfully guilt-tripped members of this crowd into buying him pints, draping their arms around his shoulders and including

---

* Simon and I once shared a sneaky Irish coffee while I was working on my birthday. I didn't realise how much he'd poured in. He sat on his chair; I sat on the edge of his bed. The mixture of alcohol and an overheated room (it was the height of summer) put us both to sleep – and I woke up slumped to the left, my forehead pressing into the edge of the headboard. I'd been asleep for 45 minutes. No one noticed. They just assumed I was attending to other residents. I said I'd got the deep indentation on my forehead when I hit my head while draining a catheter bag.

him in the festivities. And, yes, his little escapade was a massive oversight, and shouldn't be downplayed, but once he'd been retrieved (wearing a beer-soaked 'Pussy Patrol' T-shirt), I sat in the lounge with him, one hour left of my double shift, listening as he slurred along to Frank Sinatra songs that were playing only in his head, and he seemed happy in his drunken state.

With the added intake of alcohol, and because he usually had kidney dialysis three times a week, sweat dappled his face like condensation. We both sat in front of the TV: me with my legs outstretched and my new friend with his legs crossed, his elbow pressing into his thigh as he leaned forwards in his chair. (This was his natural pose, and it always reminded me of Dave Allen.)

'I didn't pay for a single drink all night,' he said.

Edgar was the same kind of geezer: full of vim and still craving excitement. He had a mind that could never grow old. Not completely. I remember one evening when I got chatting to him about his job history.

'I used to work at a hotel in Spain, you know,' he said to me, quite well spoken and tempered. As a young man he would have been a gifted salesman or seducer.

'Ah, you dark horse. You ain't told me that before,' I replied, mindlessly tapping the iPhone I'd pulled from my pocket.

'In the bar. I worked in the hotel bar.'

'What was that like?'

'Good for the women,' he said, winking.

'Ah, you absolute boy!' I replied.

'What I'd do is, is – what I'd do is … I'd do this, right. I'd find out their name. Say, Julie. Hello, Julie,' he said, waving at this imagined Julie.

'So we have lovely, leggy Julie,' he continued, 'and I'd say, "Julie. This cocktail is especially for you, my darling. A brand new cocktail. Just for Julie." And it wasn't. It was a Tom Collins, but she didn't know that. "This is specially for you – and I've decided to call it *the Julie*. This is *the Julie*."'

'They fell for that?' I asked.

'Oh, yes. Yes. And I went places with that. Lovely lady. Staying in a suite. And you know what happens next?'

'I can imagine,' I replied, 'but a gentleman never tells?'

'No, I fucked her up the arse,' he said, quick as a flash. 'I fucked her up the arse and never looked back.'

That was my cue to wind down the evening. I encouraged him to eat a couple of slices of toast, followed by a quick wash, then helped change him into his pyjamas.

Today, as I'm walking to the CTM's office in the centre of the corridor, midway between Harmony and Melody/Symphony, I notice Edgar rapping on the office window looking out onto the corridor. He's in a plaid shirt tucked into corduroy trousers. He's clean-shaven but his eyes are swimming, unable to settle on a fixed point. He appears scattered, disordered. He stumbles when he walks and drags his cane along the floor without actually using it to bear weight.

'Jeff! Jeff. Thank God you're here,' he says when he sees me approaching. (He knows me as Jeff. Or Joe. Or Pip.)

'Alright, mate. You causing trouble?' I reply, patting him on the shoulder.

'Can you get this one to help me?' he asks, slinging his thumb towards the CTM's office.

I walk around to the office's entrance and see Pat sitting at her desk, gritting her teeth, trying to suppress a rising anger. She notices me and shouts, 'Get him to stop banging that window before I throw him through the effing thing!'

'I'd like to see you try it, you fat bitch,' Edgar mutters under his breath.

'Right!' Pat shouts, pushing herself back from the desk, the chair legs scraping along the floor.

'It's alright, it's alright,' I say, playing peacekeeper. 'I'll take him to the garden for a little while.'

I gesture down the hall, indicating to Edgar to follow me.

'Come on, you naughty git!' I say, smiling.

We both make our way towards the main kitchen, to gain access to the back garden through the laundry room. Edgar is quite unsteady on his feet but, rather than using his cane as intended, he holds on to the railing running along the corridor, while the cane, hooked onto his forearm, swings with each step. He's always at risk of falling so I trail behind him. I notice his trousers are riding low, and his shirt is untucked at the back, so I yank them up – 'Watch the knackers,' he says, ushering me away with a dismissive wave of the hand – and retuck. (Old men, in comparison to the women, are reluctant to accept help. The old women are also more likely to offer it to anyone in need.)

It's after lunch. Stained trolleys piled with containers full of food waste, dirty jugs and soiled aprons are queued outside the kitchen, waiting to be cleaned in preparation for tea. During the summer months, the residents are given their main meal at lunchtime and a lighter selection of food – soup, sandwiches, etc. – at dinner time. In the winter months, as they need more energy to maintain their core internal temperature overnight, these meals are reversed. But because it's Boxing Day, and management wanted to create a sense of occasion, the residents were given *another* roast dinner – which was indistinguishable from the roast dinner they were given yesterday, and the roast dinner they're provided with every Wednesday and Sunday throughout the year. Are the people with dementia also the ones preparing the food?

The sun's shining but it's cold outside. As we're passing through the laundry, I retrieve one of Edgar's jumpers – a burnt-umber cardigan with suede elbow patches. In the laundry are three massive clothes racks. These are labelled with each of the units – Harmony, Melody, Symphony and Rhapsody – and clothes are hung up in their respective sections and in bedroom order. Any clothes that aren't on hangers (pants, vests, etc.) are placed into numbered baskets and pushed into cubbyholes labelled with each resident's name and corresponding bedroom number. (This is why residents are sometimes referred to by their bedroom numbers instead of their names – which obviously has terrible, dehumanising connotations.) Families and residents are also asked to label each item of clothing with the individual's name/number, but missing clothes are still a constant source of tension.

There's one staff member assigned to the laundry – having trained for domestic duties – and their entire day is washing, pressing (in an industrial-sized steam press) and hanging clothes (and themselves, if they stay in this role for too long). Carers used to be tasked with distributing all the clothes to the bedrooms at 2pm, after lunch, until we agitated for change. Now the laundry worker has been handed this duty as we're too busy keeping people alive.

Believe it or not, there's actually an entire book about laundry in care homes. It's called *Wash, Wear, and Care: Clothing and Laundry in Long-Term Residential Care*. In it, the authors Pat Armstrong and Suzanne Day write that the 'daily labour of laundry is essential to maintaining the appearance, cleanliness, and comfort of residents' clothing and, by extension, of the residents'.

They also identify the 'two broad approaches to work organization' that emerge when looking at this form of labour – approaches that are characteristic of neoliberalism: 'One is the detailed, hierarchical division of labour characteristic of an earlier period but reconfigured in various ways with privatization. Such an approach enhances the power and skill of those at the top while often dismissing the skill and limiting the autonomy of those at the bottom'.

This system unfortunately but inevitably results in a split between the 'worthy' and 'life-enhancing' work of the care assistants (the top tier among the grunts) and the 'titivating' or 'sprucing' work of the domestic staff – and then, even lower than that, the laundry work, which is 'understood as among the least-skilled tasks'. To characterise our roles in this way is totally unfair, but it's an unspoken division I'm sure a lot of people who work in care homes will recognise.* Under this assumption that 'dividing up the labour reduces the skills associated with the work as well as the time required to learn the job, it thus justifies lower rewards as well as a speed-up of the work. Equally important, such a strategy can increase an employer's control over the work and the worker'. With this divide-and-rule strategy, the people at the top of the hierarchy once again benefit from our misery.

The alternative approach is to create a work organisation that's flexible and, according to Martha MacDonald in a paper entitled 'Post Fordism and the Flexibility Debate', that '[holds] out a promise of more holistic jobs, a reversal of the increasingly detailed division of labour – in short, the promise of more satisfying, rewarding work for more people'. To achieve this, 'care labour

---

* This is similar to how intravenous drug users look down on the alcoholics in Narcotics Anonymous. I've never injected drugs, so I'm one rank below the IV lads, but in these meetings there's a general understanding that, when it comes to obliterating their lives, those who are addicted to opiates (or crack, or benzos) have put the graft in. Alcoholics aren't hardcore. They're just people who down Tyskies in a paddling pool during their son's sixth birthday party and then undermine their wife's opinions at the buffet table.

is organized to incorporate the work of laundry and clothing, combining it with other labour. This can mean more integrated care, more teamwork, and a more homelike atmosphere'.

The problem with organising the work in a more inclusive, egalitarian way is that, in socioeconomic terms, carers are already so undervalued and rarely have an opportunity to lord it over anyone else – so if we're to cling to even a modicum of self-worth, we have to look down on the big, lumbering, awkward boy that works in the laundry room and LARPs on the weekends. We *need* Brian. And we need him to retain a lower social status than the rest of us so we can make up rumours that he was caught masturbating in a wardrobe, in order to feel better about ourselves.*

When we channel our collective bitterness into the incompetence of domestic staff or night workers, social order among the care staff is restored.

Blame Brian, the Wardrobe Wanker.

I help Edgar put on his jumper and we sit in the sunlight, near the storage shed. He bums a cigarette from a young carer skulking beside the apple tree. I don't recognise this carer; he must be new. This is confirmed when he nervously tells me he's on his lunch break. He's fooled by my attire. The black long-sleeved T-shirt, rolled up to my elbows and tucked into my black trousers – like I'm a fucking Care Home Cowboy – convinces

---

* Brian doesn't exist. But I think we should consider recruiting Brians. Maybe it'll prevent some carers from lording it over residents.

the newbies that I'm an unspecified authority figure. And as a maladapted comedian with hang-ups about my masculinity, it's a moment I relish, so rather than correcting the false impression, I give him a nod of approval.

'Piss off, kid,' says Edgar to the newbie, along with a 'sling yer 'ook' hand gesture.

It's so blunt and unnecessary, especially as the carer gave Edgar his last cigarette without complaint. I want to laugh but I resist the urge.

'Edgar,' I say, in a tone that registers my disapproval.

The newbie meanders back towards the building as Edgar eyes him warily.

'I don't owe him anything,' he says, then takes a drag on the cigarette and exhales a plume of smoke. 'He's my son,* my own flesh and blood, and he won't even give me a cigarette.'

Edgar tilts the cigarette and stares at the cherry.

'That's not—' I begin, before changing course. 'Yeah, families are fucked. Families are nutty sometimes.'

'That's what I was asking that large lady,' he replies, despondently. 'I was supposed to be with my wife and daughter for Christmas. I don't know why they've brought in this new policy. None of it makes sense to me. Being trapped at the optician's. I was supposed to have my eyes tested and then go home – but they tell me I have to stay here, trapped at the optician's.'

---

* He isn't.

There's a stopgap quality to this care home environment that we're always trying to override. We want it to be comfortable, homely, a permanent dwelling – and to exist in the minds of the residents as such – but, to use a term coined by anthropologist Marc Augé, a lot of them perceive it as a 'dead-space',* much like an escalator stairwell, a reception area, or the lobby of a communal building (like in the 'Nether Zone' episode of *Peep Show*). Even my beloved toilets. That kind of thing. A place for them to wait, anticipating a resumption of their 'actual life'.

But a need to connect ourselves to our environment and turn it into individualised space – no matter how temporary the space we're inhabiting is – is one of the basic human requirements. And it becomes harder to attain when, as with the residents, their own freedom is compromised to ensure they remain safe.

In *Non-Places: An Introduction to Supermodernity*, Marc Augé describes airport department lounges, another example of a transitional setting, thusly:

> Surely, it was in these crowded places where thousands of individual itineraries converged for a moment, unaware of one another, that there survived something of the uncertain charm of the waste lands, the yards and building sites, the station platforms and waiting rooms where travellers break step, of all the chance meeting places where fugitive

---

* When referring to a care home, this can also be used literally.

feelings occur, of the possibility of continuing adventure,
the feeling that all there is to do is to 'see what happens.'

There's a similar atmosphere in a care home – minus the sense of
adventure. It's no wonder my nan, who had Pick's disease and was
finally admitted into a home, thought it was an airport, that she
owned, with all the flights going to America. (America was actually where she met my grandad.)

But *we're* equipped with a haunting knowledge that the *residents* are never going to fully comprehend. And as I look at Edgar,
jiggling his leg, and removing the cigarette ash by pinching it
with the tips of his calloused fingers, a thought runs through
my head and hits me like a four-minute warning: *You will never
leave this dead-space. Even if you have a trip out for the day – which
happens very rarely – you'll eventually return and be 'trapped in the
optician's' in perpetuity.* I don't even know if this thought is solely
directed at Edgar, to be honest.

Edgar finishes his cigarette and, again, uses his fingers to extinguish the cherry. We hear the distant sound of someone screaming.
It seems to be emanating from the top floor. We look up but,
between us, it remains unremarked on. Then there's just birdsong,
and the gentle rustle of leaves. For some reason the tinkle of the
fountain is absent. The motor must have been turned off.

We sit like this for fifteen minutes –

– before the stillness is broken.

'As I used to say to my girlfriends,' announces Edgar, 'we can part ways or you can part legs.'

In both the context of social mores *and* temporal stagnation – he's a man out of time.

* * *

Edgar's condition – slight confusion, a faltering independence – differs from the many residents who suffer with, for instance, advanced dementia* (or 'double dementia'; or 'late-stage dementia'; or, in the words of Tracy, 'the ones who are *proper* fucked'). It's not nearly as severe. People who are in the earlier stages of such conditions (which is the majority of the residents on the ground floor) usually have more life force, more elan, than the 'double dementias'.

The doubles[†] live on the two floors above us. It's a limbo *within* limbo, where every new day is an exhumation, a disturbance of souls who want to cut their losses and let go. Their quality of life is vastly diminished as they're incapable of much communication and rarely seem to form the kind of 'friendships' you witness between residents on the ground floor, or even respond to any external stimuli. They're like distant satellites, silently roaming the edges of interstellar space.

---

* It's a common misconception that dementia is a disease itself. Rather, it's an assortment of different symptoms caused by a disease such as Pick's disease, Alzheimer's, etc.

† I'm aware how dehumanising this is, but I want to accurately convey how carers communicate with one another. It's another negative consequence of the institutionalisation, and the time constrictions, brought on by the profiteering of privatised care.

'I imagine limbo as an extraterritoriality,' writes Dan Fox in a book entitled *Limbo*, 'without corners, windows, entrances or exits. Or a blind-black void that has swallowed all light and matter and threatens a sublime death.'

When I first became a carer, this was how I envisaged the top floor. A place in the shadows. And when I finally got to go up there, I realised it's not far off. It's confined to a single corridor, and has a languid atmosphere. Carers aren't rushing about. Everything is quieter. Some of the elders drift in and out of bedrooms or communal spaces. The rest of them are either bed-bound or dumped in chairs and pointed at the television. In the eyes of some of the staff, they're nothing but mushrooms on a log.

But some of them are genuinely dying. They're experiencing bodily death, the shutdown of vital functions, and are pumped full of oxycodone or morphine sulphate using a syringe driver. (Lucky bastards. I can't believe they're wasting the good stuff – the heavy-duty opiates – on death! It's like pouring it down the drain.) But others force me to re-evaluate what constitutes 'dying'. Or, for that matter, what constitutes living.*

---

* On that note, I'm a firm advocate of re-legislating assisted suicide and, in some circumstances, making it legal. As Stephen Sedley wrote in the *London Review of Books*, 'It has for many years been a crime in this country to cause an animal unnecessary suffering. Perhaps we need to turn our attention to the desire of human beings to be similarly spared, if that is their reasoned wish.' If an autonomous, 'right-minded' individual wishes to be remembered 'not as a tremulous and inarticulate wreck but as a whole person', why should the state prevent them from drawing a line underneath themselves?

Once I've walked Edgar to the lounge, I go to the top floor to borrow some clean flat sheets. I walk past Lyron's room, with his West Ham banner and the Trinidad and Tobago flag spread across his wall. A much-needed bit of vibrancy. I notice the upstairs carers are assisting him, so I stop in the doorway. They ask him to lean forward so they can insert the sling for the hoist behind his back. He's in a string vest, jogging bottoms and a flat cap.

'You got any flat sheets?' I ask.

'If we have, they'll be in the laundry room at the end of the corridor,' one of them replies, blowing the hair out of her eyes and rubbing sweat off her forehead with the back of her hand.

On this floor Lyron is the only resident I'm properly acquainted with as, after my first few months here, I was assigned to every floor, before finally becoming a permanent ground-floor staff member 19 months into my contract. (When I was hopping between the floors, I was still in university, and only on a bank contract, so they'd put me wherever there was a gap in the rota.) The rest of the residents have since died off and been replaced – but Lyron stubbornly remains.

When he's watching TV the carers try to change the channel before the news comes on, because the moment something tragic flashes on the screen, he lets out a grief-stricken cry, his eyes plump with tears. It's almost a Pavlovian response.

I remember the day after Grenfell. Much like now, I was bartering on the top floor: four flat sheets in exchange for clean towels.

'What's up, Lyron!' I shouted in a comically boisterous manner, a flat sheet wrapped around me like a toga.

'No, man, no,' he replied, a note of sorrow in his voice.

On the screen was the incinerated tower, looking as if it'd been dipped in Indian ink and placed upright on the surrounding common, and the ink – the annihilation – left to run down the building. Pure fucking tragedy.

I slowly unwound the 'toga' and patted Lyron on the shoulder.

'Not the day for it, is it,' I said.

After I've collected the flat sheets – and jerked the handle of an unattended medicine trolley obstructing the corridor (it's locked) – I poke my head around the door to the lounge to see what's happening. Gav's usually in there, ambling between the drinks trolley and the people slumped in their chairs, distributing beakers of juice or offering joyless, austere post-war biscuits – but not today. All I see is depleted elders in numbing repose. Biscuits left untouched on the small tables beside them. Except for one lady, who repeatedly dips a pack of playing cards in a cup of juice.

Gav is a bald, stocky 70-year-old, with concertina-like rolls on the back of his neck. He speaks in a carefree manner, with an East End accent, and is always wearing a rugby shirt and khaki shorts – even during winter.

He doesn't work here but one of the female residents here is an old friend of his. He comes to visit.

'In the past I was a naughty boy,' he once said to me, without elaborating, 'and as I've gotten older I wanna make up for it. I wanna give something back.'

So he spends most of his time on the top floor of a humid care home, fetching heavy trolleys and clean laundry from down-stairs, gently flirting with the district nurses ('Do you do home visits, love?') or escorting his old neighbour (and some other tag-alongs) to the garden.

'Go on then, girls! Get yer coats! We'll all go and smell the roses!'

He's well liked, and appreciated, by the staff. A lovely bloke. We have a few senior school/college kids who come in to chat to the residents and show them Instagram filters (including one who accidentally applied dog ears to a Holocaust survivor while she was talking about the camps) or make teas and coffees. Some of the residents' daughters (it's nearly always the daughters) pitch in at mealtimes, which is a *huge* help. A godsend, to be honest. But Gav – this stout, lumbering helper – seemed to arise from nothing. One day he was just there, in the building, holding open doors as I pushed Sylvia back from her eye test in the 'café'. And because he's detached from any origins, I think of him – in the politest way possible – as the care home troll.

As I'm trying to retrieve the playing cards from the lady, politely reminding her they're not a biscuit, Gav suddenly ambles into the room with a pile of towels balanced on his speckled fore-arm and braced with his other hand.

'You alright, darling,' he says, noticing me.

I've known a few East End types who use 'darling' as a non-gendered term of endearment. Similar to the way some African Americans use 'baby'.

I like it.

'Alright, Gav!' I reply, in a tone of voice that suggests 'I, too, am a man.'

'You courting?'

'Not at the moment. Just been focusing on other things.'

'Still doing your comedy?'

'Yeah, man! Still ploughing away.'

'I watched one of your videos on the computer. It was fucking weird,' he says, before abruptly terminating the conversation and walking back out again.

Fair play.

• • •

On the rare occasion when the stars have aligned and we have 'full staff' on the ground floor – six carers and a care team manager – three are assigned to Harmony/Rhapsody and three are assigned to Melody/Symphony. Or two in Harmony/Rhapsody, three in Melody/Symphony, and one as a 'floater' who bounces between the sections.

The formulation changes all the time in a seemingly arbitrary decision-making process. I'm a 'necessary nuisance'. And as a 'necessary nuisance', I ask for transparency. I don't blindly follow these arrangements if they're not benefiting either the residents or the carers. Though, for some reason, the CTMs seem to have gained a bit of wriggle room. For instance, a CTM might refuse a resident's request to be taken to the garden, which keeps a supervising carer in the lounge with *all* the residents – instead of just tending to an individual's needs – and frees up another one of the carers. This carer can then be enlisted by the CTM as a proxy and told to complete the remainder of the CTM's work – even if it means forging a signature. Three carers become two and the CTM gains a duplicate.

Once, a CTM – a woman who lasted only a couple of weeks – became angry when I questioned her allocation.

'There's a lot more two-carer residents in Symphony,' I insisted, 'so why have we got fewer carers?'

'I don't have to explain myself!' she shouted.

'Why? You're not God,' I replied.

'In here, in this building, I am God. On this shift, consider me God.'

'Shouldn't your three divorces disqualify you from that role?' I asked.*

But a lot of the time we arrive and hear the inevitable, though dreaded, announcement: 'Just got a call. Two are sick. We're down to four.' Or, even worse: 'It's just you and Ligaya. Domestic staff are going to try and help out.'

---

* She tried to send me home.

This is a terrible practice, but we're working for a company that's reluctant to plug the gaps in staffing by shelling out for agency staff, who cost more per hour. This is why that resident managed to get over the road at the previous care home I worked in! The most dispiriting part: Mum said this was happening back in the late eighties/early nineties too. The same fault lines that opened up and caused avoidable deaths or unnecessary hospital admissions back then are still there today. Nothing changes.

In the morning, 7am to 9am is our window to get everyone ready for the day. That's how long it's *supposed* to take to wash and dress 40 residents, split into two groups. But these are elderly people, with complex needs. Some require hoisting; some aren't ready to get up yet; some are understandably – rightfully! – resistant to being harried by other people. In the afternoon, we have a bit more leeway, as residents are visiting with their families or starting to wind down.

It's 3pm. I stack the flat sheets I borrowed from upstairs in our walk-in supply cupboard on the ground floor, and from which we stock the trolleys that we walk from room to room. They're equipped with a laundry bag, towels, flannels, incontinence pads, wipes, aprons and gloves (both large and medium). There are also small pink polythene bags for waste – like soiled incontinence pads, wipes and gloves (which will need to be changed with each resident). These are tied up and put into the yellow sacks found in the clinical waste bins in every bathroom. Finally, there are the large red soluble laundry bags – for 'dirty' laundry – that dissolve in the washing machine. These reduce the amount of time shitty/pissy/vomity/bloody laundry is handled, which helps to prevent the spread of bacteria, etc.

If we need to replenish our supplies, we find all the surplus stacked in this walk-in cupboard. Personally, I take great pains to keep everything tidy and orderly – even now, I'm putting the flat sheets in the area marked 'Flat sheets', and placing three of them on a shelf on the cart – but within minutes, the orderliness will be ruined by a boisterous staff member. (To paraphrase my dad: 'Who gets in the way of good care work? Other carers.')

'Pope – I'll meet you in madam's room,' Ligaya says as she walks past the supply closet. 'Can you bring the trolley?'

It's time for the two-hourly turns. Whenever anyone's bed-bound, they need to be repositioned every two hours to prevent pressure sores. I wheel the trolley into Emma's room. Ligaya's already in there, tying up her disposable apron, having slowly peeled the duvet off of Emma, who's lying in bed with her extremities pulled tight against her torso, totally rigid. Unfortunately, she's had an accident. Up the back, over the thighs and between the legs. Luckily the incontinence pad has kept it fairly contained. But because she's unable to move without a current of pain surging through her body, emanating from her joints, we struggle to roll her side to side or separate her legs to clean her up – to clean away the accumulated faeces.

Due to the intimate nature of the job, there are some female residents (or their family members) who stipulate their preference for female-only carers. There are also men who ask for other men. (Or men who ask for women.) But there have also been elders and family members I'm close to – Edith and Louise, for instance – who have requested female-only but with one exception: me. They know I'm a good carer. A dickhead in other areas of my life, yes. A drug addict! A drug addict who can't get his bloody priorities straight! But, putting that stuff aside, I'll treat all of these people as if they were my grandparents, my parents, or my large, wrinkled children. And they know that. Or they don't – on account of the dementia.

Ligaya and I stand either side of the bed. We've been doing this a long time, so we know how important preparation is as a time-saving initiative. A flat sheet (to cover the mattress), a towel, a clean pair of knickers, trousers, a vest, a jumper and a cardigan are draped over the bed board by Emma's feet. And as with every part of this work, some thought has gone into their selection. Are the colours matching? Are they suitable for today's weather? Will they be comfortable?

Clothing is central to maintaining appearance and to preserving a resident's dignity, so, as well as assisting them with washing and dressing, I make sure they have an opportunity to participate in the selection process, to choose clothing that reflects them as a person. With a resident like Emma, I do this by holding up different items of clothing. If she wants to wear it, she'll give an affirmative nod or say yes. And if not, it goes back in the wardrobe.

Emma likes a muted, chromatic palette. A baggy cardigan (either navy or beige) layered over a turtleneck jumper. Smart-looking trousers with a buckle and an elasticated waistband. White socks paired with clean white Reeboks.

I often think, when I'm old, Lyron's vest, joggers and flat cap combo is the look I'll go for. I don't like the chintz and frills or the fussiness you see in some old-people clothes. That's why, even now, I've resigned myself to sportswear.

The sink has already been filled with warm water and wipes. One of the red soluble bags is splayed open on the floor, ready for me to deposit all the soiled items. Ligaya and I put on our gloves.

There's a complicated choreography to cleaning and changing a resident. I've often compared it to – hear me out – the ritualistic preparation and presentation of a Japanese tea ceremony. As it says in Okakura Kazuzo's *The Book of Tea*: 'It is hygiene, for it enforces cleanliness;[*] it is economics, for it shows comfort in simplicity rather than in the complex and costly;[†] it is moral geometry, inasmuch as it defines our sense of proportion to the universe.'[‡]

You have to cancel out the noise of the buzzers going off in the corridor; temporarily ignore the list of duties piling up at the back of your mind; refuse to let needless urgency intrude on your thoughts. And this needless urgency, radiating from other carers,

---

[*] You're cleaning up a substantial amount of human shit.
[†] You're telling me! The continence nurses have to be stingy with the amount of pads they provide.
[‡] Sure. Why not.

is the biggest cause of accidents. I always say to the trainees, 'This is twenty-four-hour care. Don't cut corners or rush around trying to get everything done. That's when it becomes dangerous. Unfinished business can be rolled over to the next shift.'

As we roll Emma, with Ligaya wordlessly assigning me the task of cleaning up by handing me the wipes, I talk Emma through what's happening:

'Sorry, Emma! I know this is annoying. I promise we'll keep it quick. We've just rolled you over so I can give you a nice wash and get clean clothes on you. Hopefully this will make you feel a bit more comfortable. At least the sun is making an appearance.' A stream of mindless chatter.

Emma opens her deep-set eyes and looks back at me.

'You must hate this part of the job,' she says, slow and rasping; bubbling phlegm obstructing her vocal cords.

Ligaya encourages her to cough this up – 'Cough, cough, pretty girl!' – into a tissue.

'Cleaning up my bottom,' she continues.

We all laugh.

'I gotta say – it's not my *favourite* part of the job, but needs must,' I reply.

'Needs must' was an expression I hadn't heard until I started knocking about with 80-year-olds. Now it's been absorbed into my day-to-day lexicon.

'I mean, I wouldn't choose to do this,' she says, 'and I *am* this.'

. . .

Imagine if someone crashed into your room, slapped a cold, wet flannel on your face and then shouted at you for being angry about this intrusion. There are carers who behave this way. And it isn't always a problem with the individual. It's a problem with a workforce full of – in the words of Armstrong and Day in *Wash, Wear, and Care* – 'low-paid, untrained, and overworked staff' and company directors who are too often preoccupied with harvesting elders for profit instead of improving work conditions.

Offering poor wages and zero benefits, controlling labour market costs and staffing levels – these are just some of the ways that care provider companies inflate their profit margins. And it's usually at the expense of the workers, the residents and the quality of care received by the latter.

And since the government has been allowing private companies to take over nursing homes since before I was born (thanks, Maggie), with many of them falling into the hands of private equity, I *know* the eagerness to turn social care in the UK into another neoliberal project has led to the same reduction in the quality of care and the constant mistreatment of staff here.

Emma Dowling writes about the repercussions of privatising care homes in her book *The Care Crisis*:

The evident failures of the privatisation of health and social care services are part and parcel of the current crisis of care. For example, in 2019, all four of Britain's biggest residential care home providers were up for sale owing to financial difficulties. How have care home companies managed to rack up such inordinate debts – to the tune of hundreds of millions of pounds – which inevitably entail sizeable interest payments to their creditors? How come the responsibility for ensuring the well-being of the elderly, vulnerable and frail is being handed to private equity companies, US hedge funds and international real estate investors, whose entire raison d'être is to operate with the kinds of high-risk financial practices designed to maximise financial returns on investment? Such warning signals, however, have not propelled a rethink of privatisation, marketisation and financialisation. Instead, spending cuts have turbo-charged these trends and, indeed, created new opportunities: where cuts have hit, they have created funding gaps to which further privatisation and out-sourcing, marketisation and financialisation are considered to be the solution.

I notice these failures on a regular basis. People who can't pay exorbitant fees are deprived of access to basic care provisions. And for the ones who do make it to a residential home, they become part of a three-tier system: self-funders, those who receive local council supplementation and those who qualify for NHS Continuing Healthcare. (They all receive the same care, but you often hear management whisper things like 'Remember: they're self-funding' – which is a covert way of saying 'They should be prioritised.')

Another contributing factor to the failure of the care sector is that the companies which own them dole out disproportionate bonuses to their executives by undercutting the very workers who make up the company. Carers are unable to do their jobs satisfactorily and under conditions that allow them to maintain their comportment. They become angry, impatient and uncaring.

We end up having to rely on unpaid labour from people like Gav or residents' family members – people who feel compelled to help out because they've witnessed the breakdown of the health and social care sector and know how it impacts their loved ones.

We shouldn't be horse-trading supplies or stockpiling them so that *our* floor, *our* residents, can have their care needs met while others go without. (A recurring problem is carers arriving early so they can pillage the laundry room and hide clean towels, flat sheets, Kylie sheets (absorbent pads for washing), etc., in hard-to-find places. Or night staff stealing the day staff's supply of incontinence pads, and vice versa.)

But it's not just the scarcity of supplies and adequate funding that keeps carers from doing their jobs well. It's also a lack of basic respect for caring as a line of work.

For years I was embarrassed to say I was a care worker. The stigmatisation caused by abuse caught on hidden cameras. The meagre Mickey-Mouse-cutting-a-baked-bean-into-thin-slices wage packet. The complete deficit of support within the media. It's an occupational hair shirt. Penitential; punitive. People assume you're doing 'grunt's work' to make up for past misbehaviour.

I was fucking embarrassed of saying I cared for people.

What kind of nutty meritocracy are we living in when, socially, caring for people puts you in the 'loser' category?

Talking to other carers about the way they're undervalued by both their bosses and society, I heard the same thing over and over: no one wants reverence. Some NHS workers will tell you that vaunted, sanctified positioning can actually obstruct workplace accountability. (We all know there are good doctors and shit doctors.) All any of these carers seem to want – along with most of the key workers, to be honest – is basic respect and dignity. That's exactly what they're trying to give to those they're caring for. They give them respect, and, hopefully, this promotes an inner elevation of character within the recipient. But on the side of the government, and the directors of care provider companies, and society at large – basic respect towards care workers is severely lacking.

Whenever I talk about care work, or care ethics – onstage, on podcasts, on panel discussions and live streams (anywhere that'll have me, to be honest) – I try to be fair and even-handed when discussing the profit motives of those who own the companies, even if, internally, my ability to be reasonable is impaired by a wellspring of anger towards them. It's a complicated world.

I ask myself: When the CEOs of care provider companies talk about granting the wishes of the older people in their communities, and giving them the best possible care they could ever dream of – a rose-tinted vision of altruistic virtue, sprinkling new legs and new eyes over a congregation of the crumbling aged – are they solely driven by the substantial yearly income? Or is there truly an ethical reasoning behind their motives? And does it have to be one or the other?

Still, we have to be realistic about the extent to which self-interest prevents people from doing the right thing. It's human nature. And not all of one's personal desires, or ambitions, are going to harmonise with everyone else's.

Maybe handing care providers back over to the state is the only way to remedy the care crisis. In its current iteration, with private capital seizing opportunities created by the central government, and squeezing profit from something that should be a community service, or an extension of the NHS, there's clearly a conflict of interest at play. I have faith that avarice only plays a small role. But as a 'lowly' carer, as someone who's *seen* what happens when care provider companies 'cry poor' to avoid giving employees raises or to justify operating with hardly any staff, it's so much more satisfying to distil all this frustration down to one spiteful invective:

'I hope they die, the greedy pricks.'

• • •

Pat sometimes partakes in what seems like a weird bit of social engineering. She prides herself on the smooth running of *her* floor. And her ideal set-up is this: A few people playing bingo in Harmony's dining room, everyone sitting with a glass of juice. No stains on their clothes or food around their mouths. Hair brushed. Beards shaved. An aesthetic tidiness and a tidiness to the flow of information and activity. And, after mealtimes, everyone is transferred to the lounge and peace and serenity reign.

It's 3.45pm. Looking through the windows, I can see that the light outside is already starting to fade. And as it's the holidays, about one-third of the residents have gone to their family's homes for a couple of days, which lightens the workload. The ones who remain either have visitors or they're in bed, napping, having had visitors earlier in the day. It's fairly settled until a resident called Hattie is brought back a day early by the exasperated family friends she had been staying with.

'Does she think she's a soprano again?' asks Pat, feeling the pockets of her navy tunic for the third time, trying to find the keys to the medication trolley. She's standing in the empty dining room, hiding from family members and their endless enquiries.

You wouldn't expect it but Pat is a Christmas fanatic. In the care home she oversees all the decorating, the table settings, the alcohol (which is given to the residents in moderation*) and the extra treats such as chocolate, crisps and cheesy sausage rolls. She's even allocated herself a locked Christmas cupboard under the stairs. From January onwards she stockpiles different items for the festivities, including bottles of champagne so the Christmas Day staff can make a toast with a mimosa at the start of the morning shift. (It's one of those

---

* In 2015, I accidentally misjudged this. I got a man who fought at Dunkirk pissed on cans of Foster's. He vomited into my cupped hands. And later in the shift, he stripped his top half, gently lowered himself onto the floor and lay face down on the carpet in the corridor. When I found him, he hadn't even shut his eyes. He was just lying there, looking at the floor.

taken-for-granted communal traditions that, when you take a step back, you realise adds a nice bit of continuity to your life. Though, being sober, I now have to stick to orange juice.) And a few weeks before Christmas Day arrives, she throws herself into the task of making it special for the staff, residents and visitors. Pat is just one example of a devoted worker, committed to the care home's sustainability – and, beyond that, actually seeing it prosper – for the sake of the residents rather than for financial reward (because she gets fuck all for this).

But it's Boxing Day. She's been preparing everything in the weeks leading up to Christmas (or forcing me to hang Christmas decorations and carry tables and chairs down the long corridor). She probably has Christmas fatigue.

'Still crawling along the floor,' I reply, referring to Hattie, 'and pulling along the drinks trolley, using it as a shield. Pretending to throw grenades over the top. Usual Hattie stuff.'

Hattie is in her late seventies. Very energetic for her age. Doesn't require much assistance with personal care. As carers, we're acting in a more supervisory capacity.

If she's feeling especially histrionic, she'll opt for a black leotard and tap shoes for the day. She has short red hair, and an old-world glamour to her movements and elocution. Very luvvie. And, apropos of nothing, she'll force her portfolio on you: a CV complete with professional photos taken against a green screen.

'Look. Look!' she'll shout, impatiently tapping the cover after dumping the file onto the lap of a blind resident.

Apparently she came to acting late in life; she once even appeared as a catwalk model on *This Morning* while in her fifties. And within the home she'll conduct herself as if she were leading a drama workshop.

'Shoulders back, my darling! Shoulders back!' she'll yell at someone with kyphosis.* They just blink through their milk bottle glasses, utterly bewildered.

But the shifts in her mood are drastic and disruptive. Even her happiness is tinged with a tremulous, wide-eyed mania. And when she turns, she *turns*.

The final meal of the day starts at about 4.45pm. It's only soup, sandwiches and a slice of cake. As Ligaya's been on shift since 7am, I tell her to have a break before we start transferring the residents into the dining room. In the meantime, I'll sit with everyone in the lounge.

I walk in and make myself a coffee. There's a unit with a sink, a fridge and some cupboards, much like in the dining room. Inside is a chaos of cups and mugs and beakers. Loose biscuits. An open bag of sugar. Out-of-date National Vocational Qualification workbooks.† Even an old wooden door stop with 'AIDS' scratched into it by a bored worker.

---

* Abnormally excessive convex curvature of the spine. Submitting to my dickhead side, I used to call it – and I apologise for this – 'Quaver back'.
† It's mandatory for the care workers to have a Level 2 and Level 3 NVQ in Health and Social Care. And when I first started, I went through a 12-week induction scheme. We also have to do online training every year.

Everyone else is resting, slumberous. Their paper party hats are askew. At certain points throughout the day shift, things de-escalate. Time becomes slack and baggy (like it always is on the top floor). This usually occurs from 11am–12pm and 3.30–4.30pm. The residents with visitors have been taken to the ground-floor 'café'. It used to be a dining room but it was too small to manoeuvre loads of people in wheelchairs. The company painted it pink and white and decorated it with the tat they sell in 'Keep Calm and Carry On' shops. They also stocked it with cups and saucers with gilded edges and put out a 'piggy bank' for family members to donate money towards the café supplies. (Why isn't this included in the exorbitant fees the residents are already paying?)

In the lounge, a crescent of chairs is positioned around the TV mounted on the wall. 'Channel Three' (i.e. ITV) is always requested, but today Hallmark Christmas films are on rotation. And the residents either watch, sleep or chatter – with the noisy ones confined to the conservatory. (I don't like this arrangement. I prefer to keep choice on the table, and avoid isolating people, but during a heavy shift nobody has the time or the patience to listen to my lectures about personal agency. 'They'll go where they go!' shouts Tracy.)

Evie can be noisy so she's in the conservatory, sunk into a large pillowed chair, her marbled eyes vacantly glancing around the room, trying to make sense of her surroundings. She harangues her sister – a sister who's been dead for two decades.

'She's always after my money, that bitch. That horrible old …
my money is my money is my mummy,' she says, both fretful and
obstinate, clutching her empty handbag against her chest.

'Ah, he's being a funny boy,' says Hattie, the only one standing,
dramatically prowling towards me, ramping up to something. 'A
funny little jester. A funny little jester boy.'

I laugh.

I can't help it.

It's so pantomime villain.

'He's laughing, ladies and gentlemen! He's laughing ha-ha-
haaaa,' she announces sarcastically, drawing out the final 'a', arms
outstretched like a circus ringmaster.

Then her face darkens – again, with a theatrical flourish. High
camp from Hattie.

'Well, watch your back, *pretty booooy*' – said like a 1930s gang-
ster – 'because then you'll have no … you'll have no back … back
to basics for … you'll be back to basics,' she concludes, knowing she's lost her thread but giving a satisfied smile as if she's
redeemed herself in the end.

Nailed it.

'I'm not laughing at you, Hattie. I promise. I was just thinking of something,' I reply, checking the nutrition chart, where
we document what each person has eaten and how much they've
drunk per hour.

One of the most paradoxical parts of care work is that the
constant paperwork – the bureaucratic medium – takes us away

from face time with the residents. From bonding, from establishing a good rapport. But as a member of upper management once said to me, 'If it's not documented, it didn't happen.' And yet the very practice of documenting the incessant minutiae of day-to-day living stops us from properly participating in it.

'Writing about me?' Hattie asks flirtatiously, which makes me uncomfortable. She prods my arm with the tips of her fingers.

'Hattie! Please. Just for a minute, dear. I've got to get through this paperwork and then we'll sit and have a chat. I promise,' I reply.

'Chat, chat, chat! Chats are for bats!' she sings, flapping her arms like a restless toddler. Or a bat.

'I won't stand for it,' she continues. 'I won't stand for it at all!'

After this declaration, she grabs my coffee and pours it over my hand and the paperwork.

'Hattie! Fu—!' I shout, catching myself, but grabbing the mug and swivelling around to run my scalded hand under the cold tap.

'The beast has been best! I mean, the best beast has been breast!' she shouts, awaiting applause from her 'audience'.

Ethel, with her curly hair, and blue rinse, and gnome-like features (apple-cheeked and twinkly eyed), lets out an infectious laugh.

'There goes Dad,' she says, 'screaming his blinkin' head off. Caught 'is hand on the fork again. Poor old Dad.'

Her trademark rustic patter, occasionally splashy and unintelligible.

Everyone else sits in silence, barely glancing over to see what all the racket is.

• • •

'She's becoming a liability. And you know what will happen, dont-cha?' asks Pat, looking around to check the coast is clear. 'You know what I'll do?'

'Run it up the flagpole to management,' replies Kayleigh, another of the carers.

Kayleigh is chubby and smiley, with permanently flushed cheeks. She's very kind, though a bit head-in-the-clouds. Which can be endearing – until you find a frail old lady precariously balancing on a toilet seat, calling out for 'Nurse!' because Kayleigh's forgotten where she left her.

She has a son who's a little bit younger than me. But because of her youthful mien, and unlined complexion, I always assume she had him quite young. She's only worked here for about two years. As is usually the case, she did care work prior to this. (Experience being a pre-requisite of most jobs now. But it's the paradox of the job application: how do you gain the experience they're requesting if no one will hire you for lack of experi-ence?) Overall, she's one of those people that, when others are asked to assess her, they'll say things like 'Her heart's in the right place.'

'That's it. And then I'll convince them to let me chuck 'em upstairs. She'll be first. Barry second. They'll try to stop it, the carers on the top floor. They know what Hattie and Barry are like. But let's see them try it.'

We're in the CTM's office, the door pulled to. Pat's flicking through the drug charts on top of the medication trolley. Next to that is a thick book with the words 'Controlled Drug Recording Book' embossed on the cover.

It's 4.35pm, and Ligaya's returned from her break, so I've come to the office to ask where the thickening powder is. (Thicker liquids help people with dysphagia, or difficulty swallowing, as it reduces the risk of aspiration.)

'Ah, I think they're fine. We've got a handle on it,' I say, circling the blister on my right hand with the tip of my finger.

'To be fair – Barry keeps pooing other people's beds,' replies Kayleigh, with a teeter-tottering 'I see both sides' hand gesture.

'But they're settled down here. They know us. They're comfortable with us. This is their life down here. And you know how quickly people start to crash when they're moved up a floor,' I say.

'I can't have it,' says Pat. 'I can't have Hattie jousting me with a bloody curtain rod while I'm trying to tell Mavis's family that she died peacefully in her sleep.'

'Or Barry shouting "Enoch Powell!" during the church service,' laughs Kayleigh.

'And you know what the next step is, dontcha?' asks Pat. 'You know what will happen next?'

'Diamond Centre,' answers Kayleigh.

'Diamond Centre,' repeats Pat.

Suddenly Ligaya pokes her head around the door.

'Pope! Come and help me. Norman's in Emma's nightie again.'

I set off with Ligaya but my mind is fixed on the Diamond Centre. Whenever we have a resident whose behaviour is particularly challenging, or has the potential to endanger another resident, they're assessed to see if they require the more specialised care offered by the Diamond Centre (managed by Essex Partnership University NHS Foundation Trust). In my head the Diamond Centre exists as a netherworld, a subterranean environment way off-grid. Outside time, much like the top floor.

I do understand Pat's eagerness to pass on responsibility, even if it's born out of self-interest. She's the one being judged on the amount of mishaps or avoidable hospital admissions that occur on her watch. With that being the case, she doesn't want a Hattie or a Barry to jeopardise her good track record.

Across the board there's been little concern for what care workers need to do their job well. Because the social care sector has been exposed to the pursuit of financial profit, carers have been deprived of the levels of pay that would justify offering them further training to develop their skills and career. The knock-on effect is we're ill-equipped to face certain kinds of challenges, including residents whose conduct is especially anti-social.

It's bullshit. I've lost people I cared about to the Diamond Centre. People who needed patience and attention. And I felt I was making progress with them. Like Ayaan – short, late sixties, Pakistani. A restless, tormented soul. Always agitated and prone to flare-ups of anger if people tried to dictate to him where he should be standing or what he should be doing.

He'd always repeat the same thing to me: 'I be with you now.'

So he'd follow me around as I was completing various tasks and help me to fold blankets or make beds. To wipe down surfaces or position teddy bears on other people's chairs while everyone else was in the dining room.

We'd have brief conversations.

I remember one particular occasion:

'You came to the UK ...' I began.

'Twelve year ago.'

'Have you been back to Pakistan since?'

'Sometimes. I go sometimes to visit my family. But they give me a headache.'

We laughed.

'Do you like football?' he asked.

'No, I've never really got into it!'

'Quick football match?'

'Now?'

He dropped a tissue box onto the floor and stood by Susan's cabinets, hands turned out like a goalkeeper.

I took a few shots; got a couple of goals.

It built to a slight giddiness. And, for some reason, made my eyes water with happiness.

At the end we slapped our hands together and shoulder bumped, like boys in a locker room. He was still fairly muted but he had a big grin on his face.

'Good game,' he said.

Then he was able to sit down for half an hour without fidgeting.

In the home there will always be people like Ayaan, or Barry, or Hattie – people with cognitive impairment, trapped in a halfway world they can no longer properly fathom, and being cared for by exhausted, disincentivised workers, clogged up by a market-based bureaucracy that slowly erodes their dignity and forces them to work in such a way that this erosion extends to the people they're caring for. All the while, upper management mechanically sweats the old people for profit and – as is the natural course of things – dumps them when they're dead.*

You soon realise that, trapped in this endless cycle of neoliberal privatisation, all you can do is take off your belt and whip the heads off the daffodils that grow beside the car park. Like I do. Every evening after work.

Still – at least we have our morning mimosas at Christmas. (And they're not even provided by the upper management.)

---

* You're not going to keep them around, are you.

CHAPTER FIVE
"A PAIR OF SAGGY TITS, 66."

BINGO !

It's the 29th of December. We're coming to the end of those aimless days between Christmas and New Year's Eve. I notice the black clouds through the window; they make everything slightly claustrophobic. It's 10.15am. I'd started to transfer the residents who'd finished breakfast and taken their tablets back to the lounge, but Barry broke away and staggered, heavy-footed, to the toilet – so I followed him to offer assistance.

I don't think he's realised I've joined him. I was going to announce my presence, but I want to see how far he gets without intervention from the carers; call it an impromptu assessment to gauge his level of independence. He pulls down his jogging bottoms, then his Y-fronts, and gets to the dry incontinence pad. His back is turned to me so I can't see his facial expression, but, as there's a pause in activity, I assume he's eyeing it quizzically.

This will be the one that gets him, I think, as if he were taking part in an assault course.

He pulls it out of the depression in his Y-fronts – which are currently around his knees – and holds it up to the light.

'This is a mouse mat. A grouse bat. A mouse gat for me,' he mutters.

'I – will – use – this – mouse – mat – for – my – computer,' he continues in a staccato manner, as if he's reciting a mnemonic phrase, or a mantra, or a clue brimming with meaning.

I then realise there's a voyeuristic quality to this scene. It brings the resident's vulnerability into stark relief, and I feel almost like a scientist observing a specimen, which wasn't my intention. Having acknowledged that it's unethical to watch someone who doesn't know they're being watched, I decide to call out Barry's name – the *second* I see what he does with this incontinence pad.

He slowly brings it away from the light, looks around the room, and waddles over to the toilet (with trousers around his ankles and Y-fronts around his knees) and is about to drop it in – before I catch it.

'I was just going to post that,' says Barry.

'Ah, it's alright. I've got a post bag over here for express mail. It'll get there quicker.'

(As the pad is dry, I put it to one side. I can slot it back in place after he's finished in the bathroom.)

I help Barry to sit on the toilet, causing his knees to creak. As he's safe sitting down, I give him a bit of privacy and return to transporting residents from the dining room to the lounge.

I come back every few minutes to check on his progress. After 20 minutes, he's finally done, and standing up, fully clothed, looking into the toilet. (He's even put on his incontinence pad! For some reason, this gives me a flicker of pride.) There's a bloated roll of toilet paper clogging the U-bend – but, from what I can tell, no faeces. He continues to yank the handle despite the cistern's intestinal growl. I stand beside him. We both have our sleeves rolled up and our hands on our hips. I glance to my right and notice shit and balled-up bits of paper under his nails. Using the carer's vernacular, he's been 'picking'.

'What we have here,' says Barry, a lifelong tinkerer, looking at me and pointing at the obstruction, 'is a dog. A small white dog. A dog that's small and white, stuck in the toilet there.'

'We've got to wash your hands, Barry. I don't want you getting an infection,' I say, trying to guide him over to the sink.

'Wait, wait, wait!' he says firmly, irritated by my intervention. 'What about this baby?'

'What baby?' I ask.

'In the toilet. The toilet baby in the chair there.'

'I thought it was a dog?'

'I am *not* a dog!' he shouts.

He then adopts a fighter's stance, dukes up, ready to give me a good hiding.

It's strange in moments like this. You'd never *dream* of rising to the challenge and squaring up to a confused old man. But internally, there's the same adrenaline spike as when, in normal circumstances, two evenly matched men – or two men who are physically able and don't have dementia – are posing a threat to each other. It's an instinctive reaction.*

'No! Not you,' I clarify, 'in the toilet.'

'I'm not getting in there!'

Lord, give me strength.

'Barry. Let's wash our hands first and then we'll see to the other thing.'

I lead by example and walk over to the sink to run the hot tap. After checking the temperature, I wave Barry over.

Stooped, jaw jutting forward, and leaving a beat before he submits to my instruction, he staggers towards me. I put the plug in, turn on the cold tap as well and let the basin fill with warm, soapy water.

We stand by the sink washing our hands. He pinches the tips of his fingers together, like the puckered opening of a drawstring bag, then inserts the middle finger on his left hand into this narrow claw and moves it up and down, rinsing it under the tap.

---

* It can be funny, but tragic, when two male residents try to 'wrestle'. A slow-motion altercation. You could disrupt it by slotting a piece of paper between them.

The water darkens so I pull the plug and refill. I observe the whorls on his knuckles as if I'm studying the rings on a tree stump.

He's so gentle and considerate in this task. I don't know why I'm surprised by how competent Barry is at washing his hands. When I catch myself, my condescending thinking, I realise how easy it is to fall into the trap of thinking of the residents as only semi-autonomous.

'Under the nails, Barry,' I say, in a slightly patrician manner.

Again, he raises his fist and cranes his neck towards me, the baggy folds of skin pulled tight like the neck of a tortoise.

'I'm going to thump you in a minute,' he says.

'There won't be any thumpings today, Barry,' I reply gravely, knowing how much he enjoys doling out a good thumping.

After drying our hands, I notice he keeps returning to his pocket and fiddling with whatever's in there. I take him by the shoulders and jiggle him slightly, shouting, 'Good man! Good man! A couple of clean, dapper lads hitting the town!'*

Laughing, but cautious, he says, 'Alright! Alright! I better tell the wife we're off to town.'

His wife died years ago. There are a few photos of them together in his room. In the photos, they're far apart: him on the sofa, her standing by the door. Pat told me she'd got the impression, from the son, that it was a fraught, unhappy partnership. But in Barry's compulsion to update his wife on his plans, she's

---

* We aren't going anywhere. I couldn't think of anything else to say.

temporarily restored. At other times, she undergoes a process of full-on reincarnation and turns up inside Alice from room 18.*

'I'm really, really sorry, but are you alright to see to the toilet when you get a chance?' I ask one of the domestic staff, as I'm unable to leave Barry – or the other residents – unattended for long.

He's plump with pale skin and very short blond hair, cut close against his head. And because he glares when you ask him a question, as if he hasn't understood it properly, he reminds me of an overgrown baby. During a staffroom chat (on one of his many self-appointed breaks), he told me this delay is due to his almost paralysing social anxiety, which is further compounded by his lisp. The other carers aren't very considerate. They'll mock him (and his girlfriend, who is closer in age to the residents) and then finish with 'He's a sweet man, though' – as if that cancels out the cruelty.

'Yeah, yeah, yeah, yeah. No problem, Pope,' he replies. (I'm ashamed to say I always forget his name.)

'You on a half day?' he asks.

'Full whack today. Doing a double. You?'

'Yeah, yeah, yeah, yeah. I'm here till 7pm.'

'Ah, it's shit, isn't it,' I reply.

'Yeah, yeah, yeah, yeah. Shit. It's shit.'

---

* We've caught Barry and Alice kissing in the empty dining room. It's kind of sweet. I don't know why some carers feel they have to pour cold water on it.

There's a pregnant pause. I miss my chance to bring the exchange to a natural conclusion – or invite more questions. He stands there, holding the curved vacuum hose, staring at me.

'Look at that snake,' says Barry, pointing at the domestic worker. 'That big, tall baby is holding a snake.'

'Laters!' I say.

'See you, goodbye,' he says, fumbling his farewell.

With my left hand settled on the small of Barry's back, he staggers forward, into the lounge opposite the bathroom and the medicine cupboard. Arthur wheels himself over, a man on a mission.

'Ah, the likely … two. The two likely … ones. The one likely boy!' he says, snapping his fingers, having 'successfully' resolved this sentence.

'One, two, one, two …' says Barry, seemingly unaware of Arthur's sudden appearance.

'The clock ticketh the hour,' continues Arthur, fumbling with his silver pocketwatch in preparation for his big reveal, 'and I spy – a traitor!'

He points at me, jabbing with fury.

They've recently replaced his dentures, so he now has immaculate snow-white donkey teeth clattering about inside his mouth.

Barry puts his hand in his pocket again, retrieves five little nuggets of shit and deposits them onto the table as if they're loose change.

'Ol' Dad's been tater picking again,' says Ethel, observing Barry from her chair.

'And for the crime of perjury, I give you this!' shouts Arthur.

That's when I notice Arthur has unrolled the trouser leg tucked underneath his stump, pulled out a fit-to-burst catheter bag, turned the lever down and aimed the valve at me. He holds the bag with both hands and squeezes. An arc of cloudy piss shoots out and saturates my trousers.

With the bag drained, the final droplets falling from the valve, Arthur shouts triumphantly: 'That's what you get for sleeping with my wife, Sally boy!'

Ethel erupts with laughter.

Then she puts on Alice's coat, folded up on the arm of the chair next to her, shuffles forward, and gets ready to stand up and leave.

After a moment of scanning the room, she slides back and remains in her chair.

• • •

Why is hoarding bodily fluids – or mucking about with them – such a reliable indicator of a person's mental deterioration? There's Howard Hughes succumbing to his demons and sealing himself inside an apartment in Las Vegas, surrounded by jars of urine. Or the infamous episode of *Hoarders* where a woman called Shanna has an unhealthy attachment to food contaminated with faecal matter. As the presenters try to dispose of it, she frantically tells them, 'I'm going to go ahead and eat some of the contaminated food and then the party's over.' Getting high 'one last time' – an addict's last hurrah.*

In the care home, one of the most uncomfortable disclosures you can make to a resident's family member is that the person has experienced a childlike reversion to 'playing' with faeces, or, in some cases, swallowing it (we call this coprophagic behaviour). Initially I chose to tactfully omit these details when reporting to families, but other carers weren't as committed, as I saw it then, to basic decency.

'Mum spent time in the sunshine. Played some games. A good day all round. Oh, and while I have you – we caught her gobbling big handfuls of shite. Anyway, take care, hon. Enjoy Tenerife. See you when you get back!'

I thought by leaving out the 'grotesque' parts of the job and the aberrant behaviour of the elders, I was being a decent person. What's the harm in curating their lives and selecting which moments to pass on to their loved ones? Eventually I had a change of heart. I realised that denying a portion of their lived experience was actually doing them a disservice. This was happening

---

* I went through a stage of hoarding my own piss in empty Coke bottles and keeping them behind my desk. I was often too depressed to walk up the stairs to the bathroom. At the time, I didn't even recognise that hoarding piss was weird, aberrant behaviour. But when visitors to my university house made it clear that it was, in fact, weird, I'd place the full bottles in my wardrobe, only to retrieve them and put them back behind my desk once the visitors had gone.

– this awkward fact of care home life. And if we keep pussyfooting around it, it'll remain underreported and cloaked in shame.

In those instances, I'd prioritised the wrong person, holding stuff back to mollify the family member and preserve the uncorrupted image of Nana or Dad they held in their heads. What it really meant was that the family member didn't become inured to the vagaries of life with dementia. And if they caught a glimpse of the reality, unprepared, they might turn away and pretend it wasn't happening. This denialism can have drastic consequences; the relative might accuse us of being liars, or blame us for not adequately regulating the resident's actions. Then they'd reduce their visits, citing something like 'He doesn't even know if I'm here or not.' (Which is a veiled way of saying 'I don't want to deal with this.')

I'm not proposing we normalise such conduct, this fixation on faeces and urine. But, within this context, we should normalise *exposure* to an adult's infantilised preoccupation with faeces and urine. That's why I'm occasionally tempted to shove others' noses in it. For progress.

I don't want to seem as if I'm disregarding family members' feelings. I understand the reasons people want us, as carers, to withhold this information from them, and their reluctance to confront it head-on. And I respect their wishes. But I hope they'll try to overcome their squeamishness. It's in their relative's best interest to help the elder curb this behaviour while also divorcing it from shame. And – more to the point – we all have a social responsibility to reject any notion that may lead to the shunning of already marginalised people.

. . .

In the same way that I discard these recollections when speaking to families (an unspoken part of the social contract that should be re-evaluated), I also spend a lot of time getting rid of actual clinical waste – and there are practical reasons for this.

To mitigate the spread of disease, and as part of our standard infection-control precautions, we keep clinical waste segregated. Biological waste (urine, faeces, vomit, sputum, pus or wound exudate) goes in the yellow bags. Black bags are for domestic waste (paper towels from handwashing, for example). And, according to the 'Community Infection Prevention and Control Policy for Care Home Settings' – issued by the NHS as part of their 'Infection. Prevention. Control.' guidelines – orange bags are designated for infectious waste, and purple is for cytotoxic and cytostatic waste. (I've *never* seen an orange or purple bag while on duty.) At the end of a double shift, all the yellow bags are collected by a chosen carer – two bags for each unit on the ground floor – and taken to the clinical waste dumpsters around the side of the building, next to our garden, where they await collection by the city council.

I'm regularly assigned this job. There's a battered old camping chair underneath the roof of the bike rack next to the dumpsters, full of soiled incontinence pads. As anything that marks the end of a 14-hour shift takes on a special significance, I appreciate these moments sitting in the camping chair, looking at the stars, smelling nothing but excreta emanating from the yellow bags.

It was here I first noticed an extra part of the building, inaccessible to the rest of us. Whenever I'd sat in the camping chair, I'd stared at it, but it took me two years to understand it wasn't a storage closet or an extension of the kitchen's larder. It's a micro-office. And when I first looked through the window, there were workers inside that I didn't recognise, tapping away on computers. I still don't know who they are, or how they access this closed-off section. And I never see them anywhere else. Not in the car park or any other part of the building. It's weird, man.

Anyway – on my first ever shift in the care home, I was introduced to a resident called Clyde. He was lanky and malnourished. Any natural indentations on his face and body (his cheekbones, his clavicle) had caved in, leaving deep hollows and human scaffolding poking through the skin.* As he was mute, he had no

---

* Whenever I see a deep cavity on a person's body, I'm tempted to fill it with milk. It's the first thought that flashes through my head. And at the beginning of lockdown, I seized my opportunity. Dad was doing awkward, stocky-bloke yoga, and a little dimple appeared on the back of his neck while he was straining. I tried to pour a little bit of milk into the dimple (for a laugh) – but ended up pouring a whole glass of milk over my dad. He was fucked off. And I acted as if I was personally affronted by his anger. 'This is what families do, Dad!' I shouted. 'This is bonding!'

way of transmitting his interiority, though his eyes were always wide as if he were permanently screaming in his head. This was offset by a small, ambiguous smile that never went away. It had a disquieting effect and reminded me of Tom Stoppard's assessment of Samuel Beckett's characters, who he said always have 'a look of pity and ironic amusement, the exact opposite of laughing till one cries – crying till one laughs'.

Up to this point I'd never assisted a resident with personal care. Two of the carers hoisted him out of his wheelchair and onto the bed. He remained rigid, as if prostrate on a gurney, throughout the transfer. And because of how thin he was, there was still space in the harness for another two Clydes.

Safely on the bed, he looked at me with his wide, unblinking eyes and Mona Lisa smile. Around his nostrils were red vessels, like blood lightning, which also streaked across his cheeks. He was extremely vulnerable and brittle. The only thing that projected any sense of vitality was the quiet madness in his stare.

I was directed by one of the carers to stand on the opposite side of the bed. (The other one left to assist someone else.) I was already wearing my gloves and apron – and the black attire that would come to be my trademark.* The protective railings had been collapsed. The remaining carer asked me to release the sticky tab on the incontinence pad while he did the same on his side, and then we opened it up to expose Clyde's nether

---

* Isn't it pathetic I made this part of my identity? Like I'm the Bill Hicks of elderly care.

regions. Afterwards, Clyde made a very slight, though audible, sound – like the smallest lady yelling from inside the other Matryoshka dolls.

'We doing good, Clyde?' asked the carer.

All Clyde was able to do was shift his gaze slightly to the left.

'Good, good,' said the carer, picking up on the subtlest visual cue, a skill that's cultivated over time. The carer looked up and informed me, 'We'll gently roll him over to my side so we can check the bottom.'

As he was saying this, the corners of Clyde's mouth turned up to form a more obvious smile. Noticing, the carer said, 'Ah, Clyde's finding it funny. You gotta give the new boys a chance!'

Suddenly, an arc of blood shot out from Clyde's urethra and saturated his legs. And it didn't even look like blood diluted with piss. It was open-vein, straight-from-the-source, deep-red blood.

The carer jumped back from the bed.

'Woah,' he said. 'His dick's burst! We're gonna need a colander to catch the heart!'

I don't know what happened after this. I was ushered out. And since I was only part-time, I had a two-week hiatus before my next shift. When I returned, Clyde was gone. But that was my initiation into the viscera of elderly care and some of the primary disgust elicitors – bodily products such as vomit, pus, mucus, sexual fluids and excrement – but also violations of the bodily envelope such as wounds and evisceration. Talk about being thrown in at the deep end. Luckily I'd had experiences that had prepared me for this.

. . .

During the bottles-of-piss era, I was unravelling. I didn't partake in university hedonism in the usual sense. Yes, I'd neck 2C-B, a hallucinogen that triggers temporal distortions. I'd watch decelerated smoke expand towards a nightclub ceiling, regressive florets bound for the empyrean. Or I'd stand on the perimeter of a drum 'n' bass night, manoeuvring through treacle that wasn't there, with pupils aghast and a hammocked jaw swinging beyond restraint.

But going to raves, or nightclubs, or house parties, was just a necessary preamble to procuring drugs. A way to socialise with university dealers (mostly fun-loving types who'd occasionally reveal a vulpine ruthlessness – especially when they knew you were desperate) so I could squirrel away as much powder or as many pills as I could afford and retire to a friend's bedroom with some fellow stragglers. We'd pass around a *Gavin and Stacey: Season 2* DVD case, racked with lines of ketamine, as if it were a holy relic.

Days. The others would stay like that for days. Windows twitching and the room contracting. I'd tough it out for 24 hours, but then I'd have to bail so I could get some sleep, have a shower and re-emerge into something wholesome. Buy a newspaper. Or go trampolining. For me, there was a constant tension between leading a slack, dishonoured life and one I could actually be proud of. Between existing, slumped and dirty, and straight-backed and pure. Between illness and health.

Eventually I'd crawl out from underneath an afternoon like an asbestos eiderdown. Stale sweat gathered in the crevices. Paranoia. Attention that was previously blissful now snagging on my brain's hangnail. There was always one guy (forever coat-ready and at the point of leaving but never going anywhere) repeating jokes that had expired hours ago to try and jumpstart the good times.*

I wasted a lot of years in these environments. In pubs and bedrooms. Or public toilets. Eventually, I'd cut out the social part, the *necessary preamble*, and get high on my own.

Dirty, debased and grotesque corporeality. The biological spillage of illness or ageing. Having worked in a care home, taken drugs in toilets (both public and domestic *tips hat*) and been at the mercy of cystic acne and a tormented bowel, I've been fascinated by this for a long time. Why is something so essential, so universal, so *relatable* as our body and its secretions – as the hot mess of our somatic selves – pushed to the sidelines of polite discourse?

The shit and the piss represent a more compelling and layered phenomenon: ennui. Emptiness. We are emptied of bodily fluids

---

* I remember one particular guy who was like this. During a comedown, he kept asking me if I'd seen Chase & Status live. But I couldn't – I can't – cast aside someone straining for connection, no matter how much I don't want to engage with them. He eventually roped me into recording one episode of a podcast on Chase & Status. I still know absolutely nothing about Chase & Status.

but also drained of any life-enhancing qualities, or the motivation to even climb the stairs and use the bathroom.

And during those itchy mornings, those awful drug binges among the other druggies, and the guy banging on about Chase & Status – I remember thinking, *This must be what dementia feels like.* People you don't properly recognise, talking *at* you, while the rest of the bodies in the room seem unreasonably tranquil, and refuse to acknowledge you if you speak. You're on a different wavelength to everyone there, wondering, *Why is no one else panicking?*

• • •

It's midday. Some of the female residents are sitting in their wheelchairs, having been returned to the lounge by the hairdresser. On the second floor there's a hair salon with three of those large freestanding hairdryers, industrial basins and other hairdressing equipment. A pared-down version of a high-street place. Most of the ladies come back with tight little poodle perms. The hairdresser, who's here two days a week, is in her forties and wears body-hugging dresses with gold hoop earrings and scintillating jewellery.

With one carer off sick and the other on this unit still writing the daily obs in the CTM's office, I'm only able to transfer residents from their wheelchair back into a comfortable armchair if they're mobile.

'Looking very nice, ladies!' I shout.

'My sister's going to kill your children,' says Evie bluntly, before touching her recently permed hair.

'You are all ladies in my eyes,' says Barry reassuringly, to no one in particular.

After assisting those who can walk, I sit back down on the uncomfortable wooden chair next to the table where I fill out the nutrition charts. These have already been completed. For the time being, there's nothing left to do. I look upon the scene in front of me, with the care home's incessant alarm and the voices of ITV presenters blaring in the background – the aural detritus that pollutes my inner ear. Lunch is soon. After that it'll be dinner. Then bed. Then tomorrow. And once again I'll devote myself to the eternal recurrence of caring for the elderly.

Jill is a resident with a large, open face and a sweet nature, though her apprehension makes her jumpy and prone to need-iness and self-pity. She's part of a loose clique of women that includes Ethel and Susan W. (Cliff's wife). As with most relation-ships between residents, it isn't immediately apparent what unites them or what individual needs they are servicing by gravitating towards one another. But because Jill is partially deaf, and gloms on to other residents, they can find her dependence alienating. Whenever you're in close proximity, she'll beam at you, searching for a hint of validation and reassurance.

'You're talking to all of them,' she says, pouting, signalling to the ladies I just helped into their armchairs, 'but you're purposely ignoring me.'

'Ah, of course not, Jill!' I boom, spreading my arms wide, an exaggerated show of affection. 'I'd never ignore you, dear!'

'You are. You're ignoring me. All the others get your attention, but you always leave me out.'

Some of this is due to her hearing problems, which can make her feel as if she's marooned on an island of muffled, barely audible noise. I try to exercise my empathy and tap into the sense of separation she must be experiencing. But carers are only human. We get tired.

'It always happens to me, doesn't it. You don't care about me, do you?' she continues.

For a split second, I think, *I'd really love to tip her out the window, onto her large, open face.*

But I mustn't.

And I wouldn't.

And as quickly as the thought arrives, it's instantly expelled.

There's a book called *The Life and Opinions of Zacharias Lichter*. It's about a strange, bubbling mystic, philosopher and holy fool who spends the entire book pontificating and sermonising like a pub bore (which is why I was drawn to it). In a chapter devoted to getting old, the protagonist says: 'Old people … are on intimate terms with both life and death … Their possessions diminish (together with their aptitude for possession) and sometimes disappear, melting away like vapor into the air. Little by little old age *impoverishes* them. Even if some still seem wealthy, they all face the pure, naked, and ineffable obliteration of being.'

I like to think of death as a reconfigured consciousness rather than an obliteration – though this may be wishful thinking. It depends what my own brain is doing during any given hour. One minute I could be leaning towards *This isn't just a drawn-out cessation! There's still a chance to live!* and the next, *Ah, what's the fucking point? Mavis thought I was a guinea pig this morning.* The broken care sector, and all the accompanying problems caused by the neoliberal model of financial extraction, can place an expiration date on good intentions. Plus, the synthetic amiability carers are encouraged to adopt in this line of work tends to ebb away throughout a long shift. This is when those red-flag thoughts start to appear; those *Should I tip Jill out of the window?* ruminations.

Have you ever tried holding a feigned smile for 14 hours straight? It's draining. Not only that, but the more we carers are encouraged to cultivate displays of emotion that mask our inner lives, the less we process our actual feelings. And the more our feelings remain unprocessed, the greater our psychological angst.

Refreshing these false emotions, and being told to extinguish your private feelings, at least those that don't conform with the home's corporate interests – and doing this while walking along the same circuitous pathway, day in, day out – can make you feel as if you've caught the residents' dementia, as though it were an airborne virus. And, as with dementia, when you're stuck in this perpetual loop, you eventually stop noticing the endless repetition of your days, the once-again-ness, or remember who you were before all this.

. . .

In the established rhythm of repetitive days – a common part of care home institutionalisation, despite our attempts to break away from it – residents cling to cutlery, hide away teddy bears and take other people's bags. They scavenge and accumulate. Which is ironic because their entry into the care home requires a Franciscan-like shedding of objects, and the importance we place upon them. It's both a sad reminder of things left behind – a history of accreted materialism – and an indication of what we *should* value. Or that's the kind of trite shit I'd put forward before noticing the melodrama of stolen objects, the inveterate hoarding and illogical worship of *bits* within the nothing-days of care home life. Bits of paper. Bits of fabric. Hairbands and hairpins. It reminds me of when I was in playschool. I'd always arrive holding an item from home and wouldn't let it go until Mum had picked me up. Sweaty palm, red imprint. It afforded me a sense of security. Maybe the hoarding has the same function. Maybe – in the minds of the elder – these things have a tenuous connection to a home that's no longer there.

Games are one way of breaking up the repetition. Helping the residents unlock their ludic selves by submerging them in the temporary agency of a game. Games are motivational, goal-oriented, fun – and they encourage the players to use practical reasoning in order to advance.

I'm not much of a game player myself. I'm an eager conversationalist, so if I want to bond with someone, that's my principal means of doing so. What *isn't* part of my repertoire is playing games or joining in sing-alongs. Or dancing with a confused resident – who has a look on their face similar to the dawning hopelessness of a kidnap victim whose aggressor is starting to panic – being forced to bop and jitterbug.

'It's fun. It's just fun,' the carers insist, while visiting family members try to clap the residents back to coherence. As if they're summoning the dead.

I'll be honest with you – and you're probably going to accuse me of being a killjoy – but there's something I find uncomfortable, and jarring, and dancing bear-ish about these moments. (Again, no wonder Charlie Big Trousers drinks.)

I'll occasionally usurp the role of bingo master from Kayleigh ('A pair of saggy tits, 66'), but trivia is the only type of game I'll deign to play with the elders. Trivia is my chin-up bar. But I'll get so caught up, I'll often forget that some of my competitors have a head that's choked with amyloid plaques and neurofibrillary tangles. And even when I *am* conscious of this, I refuse to debase the art of trivia and make special dispensations for them. Not on my watch.*

---

* Which is another thing they struggle to comprehend. You ask them to draw a clock and all the numbers are bunched up on one side.

On our last trivia session, we sorted all the residents who'd reliably stay awake into pairs and assigned the role of quizmaster to Kayleigh. Sylvia refuses to partake in group activities so, as a reserve, I partnered with Susan H. (the lady with the wound on her head). We have the same effortless congeniality I share with Sylvia – plus, Susan often takes me by surprise by correctly answering difficult questions on television quiz shows.

'Bedford. His plane departed from the outskirts of Bedford,' she'd say out of nowhere in her strained, gravelly voice, in answer to a question on the historic English market town where Glenn Miller was last seen before he disappeared.

Unfortunately when it comes to trivia, I'm highly competitive. And because of this I was unable to modulate my desire to win or manage my expectations when it came to my teammate's performance.

Needless to say, I got overexcited and ended up berating Susan H. for not knowing Daphne & Celeste sang the 2000 hit 'Ooh Stick You!'

'Have you been locked in a cupboard since big band?' I asked.

I also shouted a couple of unsavoury things at the other teams. ('You're shit at triv! You're shit at triv!')

But carving out the time to play games with residents is extremely difficult for carers. We have an event coordinator whose primary function is to arrange a schedule of suitable activities, but in my experience, they're mostly roped in to reduce the overflow of paperwork from the manager's office. They become

an ad-hoc administrative assistant, and 'entertainment' is relegated to a secondary concern (if that).

The only time they might bust out the big guns and prove
they're capable of innovative entertainment choices is the day of
the Care Quality Commission inspection.*

On one such occasion, our event coordinator invited a zoo
to the care home. Or, more precisely, an assortment of animals
who were safe to gather in the conservatory and interact with the
residents. I even have a photo of an oblivious Dorothy sitting and
reading a newspaper with a docile rabbit curled up on her lap, a
couple of bald guinea pigs squeezed between the armrests and
her ailing body, and a pair of lovebirds perched on her head, nest-
ling in her fine gossamer hair (which her daughter still lovingly
styles into a phantom coiffure).

Susan W., while scratching a rabbit's floppy ears, utterly
content with her new companion, was asked if she was 'having a
nice time' by one of the CQC inspectors.

'Oh, yes,' she replied, 'on a normal day we *never* have anything
like this.'

. . .

* The CQC is the main independent regulator of health and social care
in England. It has the power to shut down underperforming homes, so
these inspections are very important – though they're announced ahead of
time. Which, to me, is a major flaw as it gives every home a chance to stage-
manage their operations, to put a bit of a shine on things. Personally, I think
there should be a care home version of 'mystery shopper' so they're always
providing the best possible care.

In 2017 I co-created the Care Home Tour with comedian Ben Target. Ben has a Zen-like mien, an embodied patience, and a reflective way of speaking that's naturally soothing. And with his shaved head, aqua-blue eyes and beak-like nose – plus his mischievousness and predilection for absurdity – it's as if he's stepped out of an avant-garde puppet show. A brilliant foil to my rambunctious Essex-ness.

The following year, we stayed at an artist residency to work on the logistics of the tour. It was a big Georgian building in Chalkwell Park. Chris Kraus (the author of *I Love Dick*) was also there for the first few days of our two-week sojourn. (She accidentally drank my can of Diet Coke.)

On one of the evenings, I turned up at 11pm after finishing a shift at the care home. When I arrived, there was a woman with severe mental illness haunting the doorway. It was cold and wet. I invited her in for a cup of tea and some leftover rice. I offered to walk her to her hostel, or pay for a taxi. Any method of getting her back safely, and whatever she was comfortable with. But she refused to leave, telling me, 'This is my house and I'm getting married in the morning.'

As far as home invasions go, it wasn't terrible. I ended up being trapped in the lobby with her for the rest of the night. She was perched on the bottom step of the staircase and I was sitting on the floor with my feet against the wall. She screamed every time I tried to leave and told me I was 'made of circuits'. She also did loads of impressions from *Harry Enfield & Chums* (which she inaccurately identified as *Little Britain*) and referred to one of the characters as 'Tim Nice but Shite'.

It's weird how quickly you can become familiar with people and forge an unexpected intimacy. Even though I was a semi-hostage, we bickered over film titles and, after she threatened to harm herself and I had no option but to call the police, as they calmly escorted her out we high-fived and both said, 'Laters, nutbag.' While she was walking away, down the long pathway leading to the park's gated entrance, I overheard her say to the police, 'He's a nice bloke but I think he's mentally ill.'*

I got the idea for the Care Home Tour after observing how residents would respond to my pratting about, and noticing the lack of diversity in care home entertainment (at least at the places I've worked in; I know there are other homes that excel at this). I realised that the residents who wanted live comedy weren't being catered for. Although, intuitively, I knew the linguistic legerdemain of a joke, or even the narrative momentum of storytelling, might be difficult for people with dementia to follow. Perhaps they'd struggle to process the internal logic – or subversion of such logic – within a joke or a story.† But during a shift, I'd boot stools across the room, shouting 'Footstool football!' or pretend to trip

---

* I was pretty gutted I never saw her again. She was actually a bit of a laugh. But, at points, quite, quite threatening.
† Obviously there's a diverse array of conditions that cause dementia – and it can manifest itself in myriad ways. But, anecdotally speaking, I've found it hard to elicit a response when telling a joke.

up and spill jugs of juice, or demonstrate my karate 'skills' (which were purposely rubbish), and I knew some of the residents found this comic business funny. It had an infectious, antic energy. So when Ben and I were choosing performers, we sought those who were adept at physical and interactive comedy and could create a bit of a spectacle. But we also wanted to combine the comedy with musical elements and dancing. We wanted the show to be close in spirit to the variety bills of the residents' youth, packed with comics, musicians and speciality acts.

For our first few shows, we brought along five other acts to do a ten-minute set each. It was still in its incubation stage, and a bit of a shambles. During one of them I introduced comedian Nathan Lang, whose stuntman act – unbeknownst to us – ended with a striptease, alarming the activities co-ordinator. His underwear was even decorated with drawn-on cock – and I was sure that was going to force the abrupt termination of the Care Home Tour.* (This wasn't vetted by me or Ben. And when Nathan returned to the corridor, to the assembled comedians waiting to go on, I said, 'Well, that's this little project burnt to the ground.')

----

* Nathan is a sweet, blue-eyed innocent. A Peter Pan-type figure. About a week after this occurred, I had a conversation with one of the residents about the show. I was concerned because she had a history of being abused by men. But she asked me to kneel down and, having done so, she whispered in my ear: 'I especially liked the part when the man took all his clothes off' – this she followed with a guarded, behind-the-hand laugh, delighted by her own candour. We shouldn't forget they're grown-ups.

Luckily there were parts of these earlier shows that redeemed this transgression and dragged the Care Home Tour back from complete dilapidation. Like Adam Riches persuading a resident to spit out a strawberry into his hand. Or Helen Duff passing around random postcards, triggering another resident's reminiscence about milking a cow in her youth. Or Ben removing a series of diminishing hats until he revealed a tiny party popper balancing on his head.

We subsequently progressed to a more inclusive approach, identifying that the main aim of these shows – which soon turned into workshops where three-quarters of the attendees happened to have dementia – was to facilitate a conversation or a fruitful interaction with the residents. Like Helen and Audrey. There'd be no more performing *at* residents. Instead (for those who wanted to take part) we'd perform *with* them. That could mean challenging a group of geriatrics to an arm-wrestling match (my approach) or introducing them to a box they could fill with special memories – only for them to misunderstand the purpose of the box and deposit their loose change and wedding rings into it. We intended the latter to spark some recollections, but it turned into an inadvertent mugging (blame comedian Joz Norris for this).

It could be as simple as helping someone to speak, encouraging them to participate or bringing them into the fold of a collective experience – and, most important of all, allowing them to respond to this minor spectacle in whichever way they saw fit (as long as it doesn't harm anyone involved).

We don't want to force happiness.

We don't want to force *anything*.

We only want to initiate fleeting moments of engagement, while recognising the tremendous value in such an occurrence for a room full of sputtering minds (including my own).

I don't subscribe to the cultural imperative to transform troubling thoughts or illnesses or life stories into 'messages of hope'. Let people gripe and moan and vent. Not everything has to be an inspirational plaque. And, to me, it's more inclusive to take this approach because you're not socially culling the participants who aren't coherent enough, or polite enough, or 'have their trousers on' enough to fulfil a narrative of 'overcoming adversity' – the kind you see in stage-managed documentaries about care homes.

Maybe Charlie Big Trousers initially had the same ideas about changing the social care sector from the ground up.

Shit.

I should stock up on Heineken and crabbing lines.

• • •

It's now 1pm. We're in the dining room waiting for Kayleigh to bring the food trolley from the kitchen. All the residents have been transferred, so I decided to take a load off and sit in the empty chair opposite Lily and Alice.

Lily is in her nineties. She can be volatile. If she's on one, she has a harsh, scrunched-up face, with little tributaries of broken blood vessels forking across her cheeks. Her hair is made up of tight little curls that reveal a blotchy scalp. When she's angry she reminds Pat of Chucky from *Child's Play*. A woman possessed. Now and then, all of a sudden, this volatility will melt into a strange, woozy calm – before abruptly switching back to anger and apprehension. She fluctuates between these two states throughout a shift.

Alice, taller than Lily, and Barry's sometime 'wife', has wide-set eyes, a fixed grin (with oversized, clattering dentures) and trousers that are usually pulled up over her small, swollen belly. Her hair is dry, densely packed and grows upwards like brush-wood screening.

Alice and Lily are always together, but only Lily depends on this proximity. You can usually find her reaching out her rheumatoid hand and resting it on Alice's forearm, anxiously surveying her face for some display of kinship.

Alice, as always, will remain aloof, acknowledging another person's presence with a subtle nod and an empty grin – except Lily, who she ignores completely. I'm pretty sure she doesn't even know Lily exists. Despite that, they're best friends.*

'I like you' is Alice's catchphrase. When she says it, it lacks any emotion, but somehow it still comes across as suggestive.

It's slightly unnerving.

---

* I know Lily and Alice as an extension of each other, a double act. Sometimes I'll find them in bed like Morecambe and Wise. Alice doesn't even know she has company.

'You're my friend.'

This is then followed by a muted chuckle.

Lily, visibly shaking with jealousy, will desperately tug at Alice's sleeve, or try and capture her attention some other way.

When we brought one of our Care Home Tour shows to where I work, we awarded trophies to the residents who participated. Lily wasn't satisfied with hers.

'Just this?' she asked, waving it at us with a limp, blasé wrist.

'I like you,' said Alice, to her right.

Lily then snatched the trophy from Alice's hand and shouted, 'You didn't do anything for your one, so I'll be 'avin that!'

She thumbed her nose and blew a raspberry, the spittle landing on Alice's oblivious face. For the following few weeks, every time I went into Lily's room, her collection of trophies had multiplied.

Back in the dining room, Alice nods in my direction – which instantly sets off Lily.

'Don't like him. He's not – you're not to like him. You can't … you can't do with liking him,' says Lily, halfway between begging and demanding. Then she turns to me, shooting daggers.

'You're a right – bastard! Fool! Blastard! You did this to my smettle!' she spits, scrambling her words.

'Lily! We're alright, Lily! We're doing good today! You know me!' I say in a sing-song voice with submissive upturned palms.

'What's a smettle?' asks Tracy, standing by the sink.

'I'll give you blettle,' replies Lily, shaking her fist like a cartoon sailor. 'Right around your prim hole.'

'You go anywhere near my prim 'ole and I'll lock you inside this bloody trolley,' says Pat, pushing the mobile medication cabinet into the room. She has a waddling gait but, as ever, arrives with Bonapartian conviction. Even though the trolley is obstructing the flow of human traffic, we all decide to navigate *around* Pat rather than asking her to move.

'And who's upset you this afternoon, love?' asks Pat.

'That old nonsense in the sink,' says Lily, pointing at Tracy while she washes up a mug.

'Oi, you! Less of the old!' shouts Tracy in mock indignation, before inflating her cheeks and blowing out some air. Wayward follicles are plastered against her damp forehead.

Pat summons me to the trolley for a quiet sidebar. Out of habit, my eyes dart to the bottles and packaging I know to be opioids. Yellow and blue for dihydrocodeine. Brown with a white label: oxycodone. White, orange and blue: Oramorph.

'If we could get this one in the bath after lunch,' she says, tilting her head towards Lily. 'She's starting to look gamey. So apply plenty of WD-40 to the face there.'

'E45,' I reply, correcting her mistake.

'Whatever the bleedin' stuff's called.'

I crouch beside Lily, who smiles drowsily.

She's reverted back to serene, tempered.

'I like you,' says Alice, leaning over her. Lily starts to frown.

'What's up, players?' I ask. 'Have you had a good day so far?'

'You're my friend.'

'And you're my friend as well, Alice,' I reply. 'Great mates. We're all great mates.'

There's a hostage negotiation, 'put the gun down' feel to this exchange.

'Oh, yes. Very nice sleep we had on the – after the show. It was a lovely show,' says Lily, suddenly engaged. 'The show was – we went to the show. And it was a show about … there were fourteen of us. At the show. And we had a lovely time, we did.'

'Ah, I'm really glad to hear it! Great stuff! Did you sing along to all the songs?' I ask.

Larissa MacFarquhar, in an article titled 'The Comforting Fictions of Dementia Care', spoke to the brilliant Penny Garner about the system she devised for caring for dementia patients, known as the SPECAL method. Garner had no medical training but, after her experiences with her mum (who had 'extensive atrophy' of the brain) and spending years volunteering with dementia patients at her local hospital, formulated her own ideas about how to engage with those living with dementia. The SPECAL method includes such rules as 'Never ask questions. Questions … put you on the spot: they could cause a person with dementia to panic by demanding an answer that they might not be able to give' and 'Never contradict anything the person said, no matter how distant from reality, in order to spare them a distressing confrontation with their own decline'. Garner also looked to a technique taught in improv courses to provide the best care for those with dementia: 'Never say no to the reality you're given; say "Yes, and," building on whatever the other person said.'*

I have no idea what show Lily thinks she's been to, so I take a gamble. I end up gently nudging the conversation along, keeping it general. Moulding her recollections in a way that doesn't jolt her sense of narrative consistency. (If a resident's historical self, as opposed to their 'care home self', didn't own a dog, for instance, I would avoid inserting dog ownership into a conversation about what occurred the night before. As carers, we don't have all the requisite biographical information. Lives are long! So this process takes a bit of trial and error.)

'I bet you'll want to hear me singing as well!' I say, adopting the persona my mum uses when she's chatting to her hairdresser. Essex (pantomime) dame. At work, in a female-heavy environment, I'll unconsciously slip into this mode.

---

* I love Garner's approach, but she's constantly had to contend with snobbery and discrimination from those in the medical establishment, including the British Alzheimer's Society. In MacFarquhar's article, the society's official position, countering Garner's method, is quoted as such: 'We struggle to see how systematically deceiving someone with dementia can be part of an authentic trusting relationship in which the person's voice is heard and their rights promoted.' How is imposing your reality and completely disregarding a person with dementia's subjective experience – not to mention the disorientation and anxiety that Alz Soc's flawed methodology will undoubtedly cause – making sure the patient's 'voice is heard'? And why would you place yourself in a contradictory, adversarial role, when the other person is protected by such 'comforting fictions'? Respectfully, I decline to trust Alz Soc on this issue.

Then I have to switch tactics. 'Lily. Let me level with you for a minute,' I say. I opt for gentle and conversational. A couple of pals shooting the shit, getting real with each other. I try to steer away from condescension.

'I know you're just about to have your lunch, but afterwards I might need to assist you in the bath ...'

'No, no, no!' shouts Lily. 'I'm not having it sink. I'm not sinking in that!'

'No, it won't be in there! You won't sink! No sinks. The bath in the bathroom. I promise we'll get it over with as quick as—'

'No! I don't want *that*!'

She points her juddering index finger directly between my eyes. Flecks of spittle hit my face.

'I completely understand, Lily. I know, it's such a nuisance. But you always feel a lot better after a bath. Shall we get you in and out as quick as possible so you can enjoy—'

'*No!* I will *not*! L-O-M-P. *Not!*'

Pat – who, like a lot of powerful people, never feels compelled to hurry – moves towards us and ushers me out of the way.

'Mrs Howland! You need a bath, so, after lunch, let's get you clean and tidy, young lady!' she says in a mock-authoritative tone.

'I like you,' says Alice.

'I know! And you're all getting on my wick!' shouts Pat. 'Lunch, tablets, bath! No mucking about!'

'You're my friend.'

'And you're ...' – side of the mouth, turning back to the trolley – '... the bane of my fucking life, love.'

Pat flashes a knowing smile. It's all done with affection.

• • •

As well as the unusual friendships that form within the home, there have also been plenty of husbands and wives who have been admitted into the home together – or, more commonly, one after the other. It usually goes like this: the husband arrives first and the wife is only a visitor; the wife is anxious and overbearing (*Pope, you sexist*) and her visits become more frequent; she starts to request an extra dinner so she can eat with her husband – who doesn't seem to like this arrangement but searches for her non-stop when she's gone; Tracy turns around and says, 'She needs to be in 'ere more than he does!'; eventually she is.

There was a couple called Barney and Iris. Barney used to be a milkman. He was sweet and non-threatening, with a childlike appearance. Think Elmer Fudd but with a tortoise shell caused by the excessive curvature of his upper back.

Barney would go outside and feed the pigeons or tend to the plants on his windowsill. In the afternoon he'd fall asleep to a western. He was settled in this environment and had his own routine. At least until his dotty wife was brought in by his niece so she could visit.*

---

* The niece then scarpered.

I'd see him shuffling up the corridor, trapped in an utterly beleaguered existence, holding on to his walking frame, a look of desolation on his face.

'Kill her or kill me,' he'd say in his quiet, throaty voice as I walked past him – followed by a wry smile.

When she was given a room on the same corridor as Barney, I'd always clock him standing by the mock bus stop in the garden, smoking beside a supervising carer, slumped on the bench, with the sun setting over the surrounding fields and the sound of falling water tinkling from the fountain.

'You alright, Barney boy!' I'd shout, bowling over.

'You alright, mate,' he'd reply.

'It's getting cold. You gonna come indoors?'

'I can't face it, John.* Even the plants are dying. She's killing the plants, John. She's killing the plants.'

I'd walk back indoors and pass Barney's room – only to find Iris waving an imaginary baton, conducting the dead bees on the windowsill.

• • •

It's 2.15pm and we're a bit late finishing lunch today. Only one of our hoists is working because the night staff (always blame it on the night staff) forgot to charge the battery on the other one. I have to keep traipsing down the corridor to check if Harmony

---

* He knew me as John.

have finished using it and then rush it back to our unit. We need to transfer the residents back to the lounge from the dining room, but as I'm marching past the CTM's office, Pat, who's finished dispensing the medication and is back to sitting at her desk, bangs on the window.

'Pope's been baptised again!' she shouts. 'Do Quakers do baptisms?'

'What do you mean?'

'I've only just heard Arthur sprayed you with his catheter this morning.'

'Yeah. Shit. Just before lunch!'

I notice that Tracy and Ligaya are hoisting people in Harmony's lounge at the end of the corridor. Tracy is supposed to be down our end, as she's been all morning, but because another carer rang in sick for the afternoon shift, she's been shunted over to Harmony.

Kayleigh, having returned from pushing the trolley back to the kitchen and cleaning the dining room, is in our lounge, waiting for me to come back with the hoist. I've got to wait a few minutes for the other carers to finish with it, so I go and sit in the office.

There are two carers – inductees – sitting behind Pat, rolling fags. I start filling out a behavioural chart (a way of documenting 'problematic' behaviours) for Arthur, noting that he soaked me in piss.* Arthur's file is already heaving with them. On the

---

* I'm reluctant to do this, as it hasn't caused me any harm, but it's in case he does it to another resident. We're constantly trying to balance our duty of care to all 40 residents on the ground floor.

whiteboard there's a small note that reads, 'Dorothy tried to bite a light bulb. Put things away!' A box of half-eaten mini muffins sits on one of the small tables. Crumpled paper liners, courtesy of Kayleigh, I assume, are gathered on Pat's desk and on a chair closest to the row of daily obs. These are organised by room number, on three shelves, one below the other.

The inductees sitting behind Pat are young. Only teenagers. Having passed them at various points throughout the morning (they were assigned to Harmony, to shadow Ligaya), I can see they already hate it here, so there's no point even learning their names. Pat strains to turn her head towards the girls and, with a smile, says, 'Did you hear that? Arthur soaked him with his catheter bag.' They laugh accordingly. But then Pat's face darkens: 'Don't just sit there laughing. Get your arses in gear.' She points her thumb over her shoulder, signalling for them to leave. They scurry out and we hear aggrieved, martyred whispering between them as they walk up the corridor, towards the garden.

'Nice girls. Good workers,' says Pat, sincerely.

'Was that legs eleven?' shouts Tracy, eavesdropping on our conversation about Arthur.

As usual, we hear her before we see her.

Pat rolls her eyes. 'Ah, here we go. Mouth Almighty.'

'Have you finished with the hoist?' I ask Tracy.

'Not yet,' she says.

I'm leaning against the door frame but Tracy barges past me, grabs the box of muffins and plonks down in a chair.

'Shut up, Pat,' she says, pre-emptively. 'I'm 'avin' a sit-down.'

She rakes back her sweaty hair with her fingers, leaving trails of exposed scalp. The muffins are balanced on her knees. She tugs the bit of uniform that's been swallowed by a belly roll, removes the wrapper from the mini muffin and swallows the cake in one.

'I've 'ad the same thing, right,' she continues, 'and we're having to keep washing uniforms and replacing uniforms and – and the other day I found vomit in my pocket! And the company don't do anything to help us or to pay sick pay or anything. I'm sick of going home and smelling like shit. I'm sick of always feeling and smelling like shit. I'm supposed to be shaggin' this new guy, and I turn up and he's made a lovely meal. And I turn up, right, with vomit in my pocket. That's my contribution. How am I supposed to feel like a desirable woman with vom in my pocket?'

We all laugh.

Sometimes I like Tracy. Especially when I get a glimpse of the character behind the casual cruelty. A person who desires and wants to be desired in return. You wouldn't expect it from her. Which is ridiculous, as desire is a basic human need, but I realise this kind of reductionism – seeing people as the role they've been assigned, or as a stereotype or a cartoon character – can be extended to anyone and everyone. Not just the residents. We don't spend enough time trying to get underneath.

'When Arthur did it before,' I reply, 'he said he had to empty his bag on me because he has a urine infection and needed to keep the piss moving.'

When Arthur did it before …

This stuff – so noteworthy in 'normal' life – becomes habitual and commonplace in here.

'He has a point, doesn't he. There's a weird kind of circuit to it,' says Pat.

'Like a lemniscate symbol,' I say, pleased with myself.

Tracy pulls a face. 'Alright, college,' she replies, legs spread widely as she slouches in the chair, flicking a flake of dried skin she's peeled from her elbow. 'Try and lemon biscuit your way into a vagina once in a while.'

She then turns to Pat, who's back to her paperwork, and says, 'Pat. Did you hear what I just said to Pope?'

'Finish up with that bloody hoist. You're late as it is,' replies Pat.

. . .

Baptism is meant to cleanse the person of sin and bring them into alignment with the sanctification of God's kingdom. And whenever a resident has a bath there's usually a subtle transformation and sense of relief. It's as if they were uncomfortable but couldn't quite put their finger on the cause of this discomfort until they underwent this ablution ritual. Even Lily – who is violently opposed to having a bath whenever the issue is raised – emerges from the bathroom speaking in half-whispers with a dreamy expression on her face. And if cleanliness is next to godliness, something as earth-bound as shit or piss has no place in this symbolic system.

But, as we've already seen, there's a democratisation, a humanistic quality, to matter issuing forth from the body's orifices. It binds us – but it can also upend the social order. And talking about it, or writing about it, puts one at risk of social pollution.

The management in *another* place I worked tried to introduce a new policy where bathroom breaks were timed. Frankly the last thing I needed was for administrators and micro-managers to draw attention to my awkward toilet habits. But because they did, and because they insisted on enforcing such rules without deigning to discuss the finer points of their decrees,* I photographed my shit, printed it out, affixed a label with the amount of time I'd been in the toilet for (using my iPhone's stopwatch) and pinned it to my manager's door.

People were blindly acquiescing to this invasive, dehumanising rule, so I made it *very* real – and the practice stopped.† You know what they say: you can't make an omelette … with shit. That's the saying.

This stuff is a tough sell. Shit and piss and all that. I sometimes make it part of my stand-up set. Shit teeter-tottering on my sphincter. Giving myself an enema with a marker pen. Bottles of piss. Diabetic ulcers.‡ But it's a sure-fire way to divide a room.

---

* As someone with a chronic bowel condition, I tried to raise the issue with them but it fell on deaf ears.
† Along with my contract.
‡ I also do nice stuff about a bin man, the Amish and saving a worm.

As a comedy trope, child abuse meets more approval than faeces or any other bodily degradation. Some may say it's foolhardy to talk about such things when it causes division between me, the comedian, and the audience I'm trying to win over, when it's so antithetical to the unification and the cohesion a comedian is trying to achieve.*

But we all expel bodily fluids, and cast them aside; the very act of surrendering our waste is a vital feature of our lived experience. And it should, in some weird way, bring us together.

We shed this material in order to live, and once it's purged from our bodies and turned into non-living material, we're reminded of our own mortality, of the time when we'll finally be cut asunder and float into the dark. (Well, that's what *I'm* reminded of.)

We all need to get on board with this stuff, and stop being so uptight, so others aren't left behind. As Penny Garner said in response to those who took umbrage with her methods – who 'worried that to lie was to betray a trust' – 'Grow up'.

'All these convexities and orifices [the anus, the genital organs, the mouth] have a common characteristic,' writes Bakhtin, in *Rabelais and His World*.

It is within them that the confines between bodies and between the body and the world are overcome: there is

---

* According to her *New York* magazine profile, Michaela Coel 'once wrote a blog post about people who talk about poop and those who don't; she is firmly in the former camp'. I'm in good company!

an interchange and an interorientation. This is why the main events in the life of the grotesque body, the acts of the bodily drama, take place in this sphere. Eating, drinking, defecation and other elimination (sweating, blowing of the nose, sneezing), as well as copulation, pregnancy, dismemberment, swallowing up by another body – all these acts are performed on the confines of the body and the outer world, or on the confines of the old and new body. In all these events the beginning and end of life are closely linked and interwoven.

As the *old body* starts to leak, especially if it belongs to someone we're on intimate terms with, it can be hard to reconcile the person you knew with the one that sits before you. We're not conditioned to witness such a display, so it seems like a confrontation. Arthur is still a well-turned-out, dignified man. He polishes his tie pin with spit and a bit of elbow grease. His ability to command a room has hardly waned, and he's endowed with the same authoritative bearing as when he was *new* (or newer/new-ish). But his mind – his poor, febrile mind – leads him into situations where he's hosing me down with the contents of his catheter bag.

When people see this, and hear the myths about, say, the 'box of Maltesers that contained something other than Maltesers', they turn away or try to brush it under the carpet. They delude themselves into thinking it isn't happening. And that kind of self-preservation is totally understandable; we all do things to mitigate the harm that circumstance inflicts upon us. But when comedians, writers, film-makers, or other such artists offer a sanitised representation of ageing, of care homes, it deprives us of the uncomfortable realities of this denouement. And this is when marginal figures are first forced into that role, and rejected from the social body.

So, yes, let's raise our bottles, or catheter bags, or colostomy bags, and make a toast for the universality of abjection! Hear, hear!

CHAPTER SIX

ARE ALL OF THESE DEAD OR JUST SOME OF THEM?

The disjunction between a care home entertainer's forced merriment and the reception they get from the residents (a reception that ranges from total apathy to vague comprehension) is always soul-destroying. The veterans of the care home circuit (Charlie Big Trousers, for instance) pretend they're braced for it, that they're driven solely by philanthropy or a misguided altruism, and that the small flashes of engagement make it all worthwhile – but, truth be told, they don't. Ultimately, all care home entertainers need to cultivate a robust denialism ('It's fine! They're loving it!') if they're going to carry on.*

I remember a performance in another care home. It was 3.30pm. Outside, the light of midwinter was fading, and there was a concomitant gloom that sank the spirits of those gathered inside the tiny, musty lounge. To add insult to injury, there'd been a power outage during the first five minutes of the (and I mean this in the loosest possible sense) show. All the maintenance man could find to illuminate the performer was one solar-powered torch, which he propped up on a pile of dementia pamphlets and pointed at the microphone stand.

In this eye-straining half-light, the performer was wearing a cape over his sweatshirt and jogging bottoms.† And as the 'show' resumed, he pretended to square up to a rubber egg dangling from a piece of string, which he headbutted as if he were playing a game of tetherball. All of this was accompanied by a happy hardcore remix of Vera Lynn's 'We'll Meet Again' – because he thought he'd try something different, and that care home audiences shouldn't be excluded from diversity in the arts. But after the show, while removing the cape and packing away the egg,

---

* When I spoke to a local newspaper about one of our care home comedy shows, I said: 'I'm thrilled at that. You probably couldn't tell, but people were bloody loving it.' They weren't. I was lying. But I didn't have the balls to provide an honest evaluation, to own up to the fact that, in this early stage, our project had little to no value. Still, it's better to try something than do nothing at all. Except on that one particular occasion.
† The sweatshirt had the words 'OLD IS FUN' stitched onto the front.

he realised the majority of the audience didn't even know they'd spent the last 20 minutes watching their guest headbutt an egg. What was he thinking? Why did he wear a cape? Why did he choose happy hardcore for a group of geriatrics? Why did he opt for the headbutting-an-egg bit, even though he'd only thought of it on the car journey to the home? As he was about to leave through the main entrance, utterly hollowed out by the experience, the strip lights buzzed back to life and illuminated the faces of the elders – faces that looked like wet laundry draped over a radiator. Nobody said goodbye.

(Hands up – that performer was me. There was also a bit where I got flustered and spoke earnestly about the perils of alcoholism.)

The border between expectation and reality, or between these two irreconcilable tempos (dead-eyed elders confronted by a bad avant-garde performance), has a lot in common with New Year's Eve. Out of all the holidays, I find it to be a sad and anticlimactic occasion, despite its spangled veneer. I know I'm not the only one.

Maybe this is part of the reason we don't really celebrate it in the care home. The desperate death-cult clowning. The nothing response from the elders. These are hard to take on any normal day of the week, but they'd be especially bleak with the backdrop of New Year's revelry. Bleak and slightly hysterical. Like a grieving parent passing around party hats, forcing family to celebrate her dead son's birthday with a game of KerPlunk. That kind of thing.

Putting my pessimism aside for one moment, there *are* opportunities for us all to fuck about and indulge our playful side in the care home. But if it's going to be worthwhile – or, best-case scenario, moderately enjoyable – we need *some* engagement, *some* reciprocity. A way of capturing their attention. And creating the right conditions is difficult when most of the audience is in the midst of a slippery, untameable madness, with many shades of diagnosis and ways of exhibiting their unreason.

It's ironic that dementia can disrupt the staged absurdity. In comedy – *some* comedy – there's a looseness and latitude of living that overlaps with the effects of dementia. You'd think they'd complement one another.

'It is through comic obscenity that we triumph over the body's mortality,' writes Howard Jacobson in *Seriously Funny*. 'Where the body dies and its deathfulness is mocked, there it is reborn. The same process works for all our passions. We gain ascendancy over what is vile in us by relishing it with coarse laughter.'

But when you have the self-aware eccentricity of a comedian – a construct, of sorts – going up against the authentic illogic of demented behaviour, the former is always going to be beaten by the latter; by the absurdity of the human condition present in care home life. In the care home we find a natural, *organic* Theatre of the Absurd, where nutbags* are free of self-reflection and self-consciousness, their brains having escaped the leash.

---

* I use this as a term of endearment.

Comedy performance is madness with the safety wheels on. You can't go full-on nutty fuck. Or you can but – if it's a care home show – you risk frightening a room full of elderly people and inducing a couple of heart attacks.* Even when performing at a comedy club, there are still unspoken boundaries. They may be mutable, situational and contextual, but they exist, and it's my job, as a comedian, to determine where the verbal trip hazards are situated and how far I can take a joke. Through trial and error a consensus is eventually reached on the terms of the social contract. The 'demented' elders, on the other hand, can do as they please. They're partially liberated by the illness – but at such a drastic price. (And it's my job, as a *carer*, to find the physical trip hazards on the residents' behalf. But I'll only police their speech and behaviour if it's impacting another resident or putting their own health at risk.)

Another possible reason for my care home's reluctance to celebrate New Year's Eve: it symbolises – like Jacobson's 'triumph over the body's mortality' – rebirth and rejuvenation, an unsuitable message (or a very belated message) for those who are trudging along on borrowed time. But it could be some of the residents' last opportunity to see in a new year, so it's a shame we don't mark the occasion like we do with other holidays. Maybe by giving them a couple of extra painkillers to go nicely with a glass of wine? Or passing around the syringe driver full of morphine?

----

* 'They're crying with laughter. Look at 'em! They're panicked screaming with laughter. Can't get enough of it! They're terminal cancer with laughter, this lot.'

(Then we could all have a go on it. Not just the greedy, selfish terminal patients.)

Today is New Year's Eve. I'm working. And it isn't much different from any other shift, except a new resident has arrived from the local hospital. As it's only 8.45am, it's still quite early, and inconvenient, for a new intake, but apparently he's 'with it' – or doesn't suffer from any neurological disorders. He's recently had his gallbladder removed, which is why he's arrived in a flimsy hospital gown, barely concealing his penis. During handover, Pat felt she had to forewarn us, in a hushed, furtive tone, that 'he has a moustache'.

'Why's the moustache a secret?' I asked, post-handover, when she told me to sort out his induction.

'Data protection,' replied Kayleigh. She was holding the small transparent pots we use to dispense the medication. (It's a bit premature as she's only halfway through her NVQ Level 4 qualification for middle managers.*)

'That's not data protection,' I said.

---

* I'm often asked to consider moving up the ladder. Through extracurricular reading, I've acquired some of the knowledge. And, according to colleagues, I have the right temperament. But I always refuse for a couple of reasons. Firstly, I own a baseball cap that says 'I Heart Oxycodone' on the front of it. If I had such easy access to drugs, I *would* steal them. No doubt in my mind. I've sucked on a handful of cat litter because it was soaked in Oramorph, for Chrissake. I know myself! Secondly, as mentioned, the higher you ascend within the corporate structure, the more detached you become from the needs of both the staff and residents.

'We don't want to take any chances,' responded Pat, leaning in and glancing from side to side. 'He has a moustache and let's keep it at that.'

Standing at the doorway of room 27, where Larry, the new resident, will be temporarily based (he's only here for what they call 'respite care' so he can recover from his operation, probably due to patient overflow at the hospital), I notice that he has, indeed, got a moustache. A lovely one as well. Thick and peppery.

He's sitting in an armchair, flanked by two paramedics who still haven't covered his bottom half. His ball sack has spilled onto the cold leatherette chair, looking like the aftermath of a mudslide. They're checking his blood pressure. I drape a blanket over his legs. Outside it's grey and wet. The rain falls diagonally and I notice the drops rolling down the window before fusing together, tumbling into one.

There are plenty of paramedics who are diligent, hardworking professionals, remaining cool under pressure regardless of the situation. I have all the respect in the world for them. And when they're met with incompetence from carers, they swallow their frustration, knowing it'd only distract from their duty of care towards the patient. But there are also some who arrive at the home with a need – a pathetic, adolescent need – to promote their status as life preservers while simultaneously diminishing a carer's place in the world. And, anecdotally speaking, they're always men.

There's one of each beside Larry.

'You can see what's happening, can't you?' says one of them, curtly, looking up from the BP cuff squeezing Larry's left bicep. He holds eye contact with me. He's middle-aged, with a shaved head and a grey goatee. At approximately six feet, he's an inch shorter than me. (Gutted.)

'Yes. Don't mind me. Crack on with whatever you need to do. No rush, no rush,' I reply.

'I know there's no rush,' he responds, looking down again to fill in a chart. 'I don't need you to tell me that.'

The other one looks at his colleague, then looks at me and gives a reassuring smile. He's young and clean-faced.

'I'll ask again – you can see what's happening, can't you?'

'Yes. You're checking Larry's vitals,' I answer, biting my tongue.

'Correct. So why did you interrupt and put the blanket on his legs?'

'Larry,' I say, 'really nice to meet you, by the way. I'll chat properly in a minute, but I just wanted to ask – you didn't mind me covering you up, did you?'

'No, not at all,' replies Larry with a chuckle. 'It was getting rather chilly.'

'I thought it might be a bit uncomfortable with your ball bag flopped out.'

Both Larry and the young paramedic laugh.

'We were working and you put the blanket on his legs. It's disruptive,' says the middle-aged paramedic, straightening his back.

'How exactly?' I ask.

'A hundred and forty-five over ninety,' he says to the young one, ignoring my question.

I let it go.

What he didn't anticipate is this: I have an unearned sense of superiority, and if I pair my ego with the insecurities generated by (a) the devaluation of care work and (b) having been a sexually inadequate teenager, I'm able to achieve a psychological homeostasis. And at this point of balance – with the twin poles each carrying a charge – I feel emboldened to turn to the older paramedic and say:

'Actually, it's a hundred and forty-seven over ninety.'

'What's that?' asks the paramedic.

'You read it wrong. It's a hundred and forty-seven over ninety. Good job I was here to clock it.'

'It doesn't matter. The difference between them is negligible,' replies the paramedic, trying to affect an air of disinterest. Whatever he has to do to appear unruffled.

'You're alright, aren't you, Larry?' he suddenly shouts, roughly patting Larry on his shoulders, hard enough to make him wince.

'He's alright,' I say, moving closer to Larry, 'but when it comes to your medical records, would you prefer it if they're right – or almost right?'

We now have a hand resting on each of Larry's shoulders. Me on the right, the senior paramedic on the left. (The younger paramedic is out of the way, crouched in the corner of the room, looking at another monitor and taking notes.)

'Oh, I suppose—' Larry begins, before his response is abruptly terminated by the older paramedic.

'Can unauthorised personnel please leave the room,' he says, whipping the blanket off Larry's legs and shoving it in my direction.

'It's so weird it was actually a hundred and forty-seven over ninety, though,' I say, a final parting shot. 'Again, thank God I was here to catch it.'*

Once the paramedics have left, it's just me and Larry. Ordinarily there'd be two carers in the room for an induction – or that's how many there *should* be – but as there are only two carers overseeing the whole of Melody/Symphony (excluding Kayleigh, who's been 'borrowed' by the CTM) and 12 residents that still need to be assisted with personal care before being taken to breakfast, I don't know how we can possibly make this work.

I'm paired with Ligaya. If Ligaya stopped helping other residents with washing and dressing, and came to room 27 to supervise as I make an itinerary of all Larry's belongings, and conduct a physical examination to check if he has any bruises or abrasions (which will be logged on a 'body map'[†]), we'd be delayed by about 30 minutes. And if we also factor in the inherent unpre-dictability of human behaviour, and the slow movements that are

---

* Yes. Very petty. But I couldn't resist.
[†] Body maps are in the daily observation folders. There's a diagram of human anatomy, both front and back, for us to draw on any marks etc. we find on their body, along with a brief description ('A small graze on the left knee; raised and slightly red; no blood or leaking fluid') and the date/time we discovered it.

a defining characteristic of the aged, the knock-on effect would mean breakfast wouldn't be served until nearly 10am. And this would lead to increased agitation among the residents, a reprimand from our manager and complaints from family members. You see what I mean? You see how we're expected to perform impossible tasks with a phantom workforce?

And as Larry is a new arrival, these administrative duties can't wait. If he's covered in marks, having been manhandled by hospital staff, and these aren't documented upon his arrival, we'll be blamed for them by the hospital. And even though we should be part of an interlinking network of welfare and dependency – a matrix of beneficence, where respect goes both ways – there's a constant war of attrition between care homes and hospitals. Hospital staff assume care homes are full of unprofessional, incompetent workers. And carers resent the hospital staff for not recognising their role in fulfilling the care requirements of their residents. As a result, both institutions are always trying to pin the blame on each other instead of owning up to their failings or taking comfort in the commonalities of healthcare workers. Mutual support is almost non-existent.

Larry and I go through the usual pleasantries as I begin the process of ingratiation. I prefer it to be a natural and spontaneous communication rather than a commercial distortion of the heart so I ask him about stuff I'm genuinely curious about. Personal stuff. The common plot lines of his life story and the vast territory of his inner spirit.

'You ever been in a fight, Larry?'

'When I was a young man, perhaps. But I never was much of a fighter. I'd rather use my words than my fists.'

I instantly warm to a person if they're unfazed by an out-of-left-field question and answer without skipping a beat.

'How about you?' he continues, sticking with this digression.

'I've never *won* a fight. But, yeah, I've had quite a few.'

'Sweep the legs or go for the groin,' he replies.

We both laugh. Fifty-five years separate us, but we're still capable of performing these rituals of male bonding. Chatting about fights. Trading some fight tips. Making a joke about groins.

The physical examination isn't meticulous, just a quick scan of his naked body. I'd usually do this after politely asking the resident to lie down on the bed, or hoisting them on top of their duvet, but Larry is pretty mobile, and only requires help standing up and sitting down while holding on to his walking frame. In order to protect his privacy, I draw the curtains and shut his bedroom door, and ask him if he's comfortable for me to perform the check while he's standing next to the armchair.

In this kind of situation, the resident is in an extremely vulnerable position; they're almost giving themselves over to the will of another person (and, at this point, to someone they barely know). It must be nerve-racking. And even if it's now commonplace for me to observe ageing bodies when washing and dressing a resident, Larry's probably feeling incredibly exposed and requiring reassurance.

Here's another negative impact of critical staff shortages: wicked people taking advantage of a situation where they're alone with a vulnerable person, where the vulnerable person is at the mercy of a stranger's intentions. There's a disproportionate physicality between Larry and me. Imagine how much more vulnerable he'd be if his ability to interpret events were automatically questioned due to his dementia.

Luckily I'm a fairly decent person. Of course I've been a dickhead at certain points outside of my role as a carer. I've been rude, selfish, obnoxious and hateful. But I also have strict ethical ideals that preclude me from inflicting harm upon a person I'm caring for or, more broadly, purposely hurting *anyone* I encounter.

I like to think there's a strong moral underpinning to my conduct. It comes with the territory. And if you allow yourself to be influenced by care work, the crystallisation of your moral centre should be a natural consequence of looking after people. But imagine what could happen if Larry were left alone with someone who wasn't 'fairly decent' and had allowed darkness to prevail?

'I once got an acorn stuck in my belly button,' I say to Larry, who's now fully dressed and sitting back in his armchair, to revive our conversation and continue the induction.

· · ·

I remember when Hattie first arrived in the care home. She was unlike a lot of the new intakes in that she wasn't cautiously assessing her surroundings, or punctured and bruised from a hospital stay that preceded her arrival. She was totally self-possessed, and walked ahead of her children as they made their way up the corridor, before introducing herself, then introducing her children.

'So, young man, we'd like to be shown to our seats as we're here for the … for the, erm …' she said, betraying her tenuous grip on reality, but still speaking with conviction. 'Well, no need to tell you! You know why we're here!'

She then clicked her fingers in front of her daughter's face and demanded a cigarette.

'Smoke, don't smoke,' she continued, holding her hand out in anticipation of the cigarette, 'we're all gymnasts, aren't we!'

Pat spoke to the family, away from Hattie, while I made this 'gymnast' a tea in the lounge. She sauntered across the room, towards the conservatory, and surveyed the residents, who were in their chairs napping, or staring at the TV, or phantom-knitting/ phantom-hemming/phantom-folding.

'Are all of these dead or just some of them?' she asked, raising her eyebrows and moving her splayed hand in a circular motion to indicate 'all the people in this room'. A genuine enquiry. 'What's the present situation?'

'No, none of them are dead. It's the morning lull, so they're relaxing,' I replied. 'Some of them are in the other dining room, playing bingo.'

'No, thank you,' she scoffed. 'Bingo's for old people.'

She then walked over to Edith, who was still mobile at this point, and able to talk, though often confused and disorientated.

She had pillows slotted between the armrests and her delicate torso to keep her in an upright position, with another pillow turned vertically and positioned behind her head and spine.

She slowly turned her head to Hattie. Her eyes were magnified by her milk bottle lenses. She blinked, sniffed, and crumpled her brow, curious about this sudden spark of noise and motion.

Hattie rapped on Edith's glasses with her knuckles.

'Knock, knock, knock,' she said, in time with the action, causing Edith to jerk unexpectedly. 'And aren't you a curious little thing.'

'Oh, yes, I think I'm ... I think I'm not sure,' replied Edith, in a timid librarian whisper.

'I was just checking you aren't dead, dear!' shouted Hattie condescendingly, over-enunciating every word and crouching with her hands on her knees.

'Oh, no, I'm ... I'm here. I'm here,' murmured Edith.

Hattie strode over to the unit where I was making the tea and hit me on the back of the shoulder.

Afterwards, with a theatrical speaking-behind-her-hand gesture, as if engaging in a private conversation (but one overheard by everyone else), she said, 'Yep. The little bald one's dead. Better wheel her outside. Looks like we've got a lot of work ahead of us.'

There was a pause; we both held eye contact.

She then followed this with a hand squeeze – as if to convey 'You're doing a great job' – snatched the bag of sugar next to the kettle, put it in her coat pocket and moseyed off, out of the room, without saying another word.

When Larry arrived this morning, he didn't have any family members escorting him to his new accommodation. He was free of guilty children acting as vectors for anxiety. I see this a lot with the relatives. It's an anxiety born out of both genuine worry and a barely concealed resentment. The resentment is most apparent with the men, who sigh impatiently as the women ask follow-up questions, or repeatedly check their watches, unable to comprehend why they've been forced into the 'feminine' arena of care provision.

It is a permanent thorn in the side of some middle-aged men. And it's occasionally channelled into short, sharp comments that they direct at carers – especially male carers. For we represent the cowed, castrated male who's willingly taken on a 'woman's role' – which means they're expected to take on some of that as well.*

Unencumbered by the baggage of sons and daughters, Larry also has few possessions, even by a new arrival's usual spartan standards. But there's a compact leather doctor's bag in the corner of the room.

———————

* I seem to be in a permanent struggle with middle-aged men. Or a certain type of middle-aged man. 'Mauve-collared drinking men' as Jacobson describes the typical Embassy Club audience. (My dad told me they had a CID training centre near there in the eighties and nineties, so it was always full of coppers.) I want them to accept me, but they never do – and, for that reason, I must destroy them. Maybe that's why I always end up in an intellectual cockfight with these surrogate dads.

'Is that all you've got with you, Larry?' I ask, pointing towards the bag.

'Ah, yes. I meant to ask you about this. See – these are some of the essentials I put in my bag before going to the hospital. I'd like to keep hold of them, if I may.' (Larry's well spoken. I've only just noticed. And as soon as it registers, I regret telling him about the acorn.)

'I'm sure it'll be alright,' I reply, 'but it depends what's in there. There are residents who wander into other people's rooms and we can't guarantee everything in here will be secure. Is it alright if I have a butcher's? I have to document it as well.'

'Of course. Go ahead,' he says, as gracious and accommodating as he's been throughout our interaction.

I walk over to the corner of the room, collect the bag and ...

Drugs. The bag is stuffed with drugs.

There's non-psychotropic medication. The kind that lowers cholesterol or prevents blood clotting, that unclogs the tubes and cleans out the vents without reconstructing the neurocircuitry of one's brain. But then there's the good shit, the stuff that truly transforms one's core self or identity.

As an addict, I quickly spot what Larry's hoarding: morphine sulphate (200 mg); diazepam (10 mg); zopiclone (7.5 mg); dihydrocodeine (40 mg). And at this point I fall away from myself. The world recedes and nothing exists but those tablets. The consequences won't matter because if I were to neck some of the dihydrocodeine and diazepam or crush and snort the MST, I would be reconfigured in the most fundamental, existential way.

Suddenly seeing all those drugs, so unexpectedly, was a shock. It took me back in time five years, back to the height of my own substance abuse, where I'd be downing Coke laced with morphine while travelling to work. It calmed me. It helped me to achieve a sense of connection with others. It gave me what I needed to get through a shift – 14 hours of smelling the rough, raw groins and buttocks of elderly people caked in shit. Those poor people. Without *something* in my system – without the revelation of interconnected-ness that opiates summon forth – it'd be too much to take.

This loss of connection I felt – the loss of control and the deep, abiding discomfort I felt with myself – was partially a result of being seen as an unskilled and disposable care worker within the corporate structure. If upper management adopted the correct concept of care – one that's collective, skilled and sociable – maybe I would have given up the drugs even sooner.

I'm clean now. And even better at my job. And I've got too much clean time to reset the clock. I last used in 2017, before I went to rehab. (Actually, I relapsed a couple of times after rehab. The recovery narrative is never that tidy.)

The bag sits open on my lap as I'm perched on the edge of Larry's bed. He has no idea of the crisis he's accidentally set off inside my head. But I manage to place the bag on the floor, leav-ing everything as I found it, and excuse myself. I walk to the staff bathroom, sit on the toilet and watch a few minutes of *Inside the World's Toughest Prisons* on my phone. Once the need has quietened, I go and find Pat to tell her about Larry's bag.

• • •

I was escorted to an empty, but comfortable, room that contained a TV, a desk, a bath and a serviceable bed, like a budget hotel you'd find just off the city centre. The kind of room I slink back to after a gig and a midnight writing session in a Wetherspoons, while nursing a Diet Coke, utterly alone.

This was in February 2017. Despite rehab's neutral surroundings, and the generic warmth of the bedroom, everything felt loaded and vaguely punitive. Mum sat with her bag on her knees. Dad stood the way my brother and I always stand: upright, chest forward, the backs of our wrists pressing into our hips, with our hands turned outwards. A slightly effete Superman.

I was the one to blame for this, for my life's derailment. So I felt shame. And I passively received the staff's introductions and a housekeeping speech delivered by a man named Napoleon. Swear to God, Napoleon.*

There was a distinct juxtaposition between Napoleon's speech about 'sanctuary' and 'restoration' and the fact that my toiletries were being searched for razor blades and my belt and shoelaces stored in Ziploc bags.

---

* I respect the fact he didn't draw attention to it, but I was fascinated by this unspoken detail. You'd think he'd at least mention it. Maybe he's spent his whole life mentioning it and wants to exist without a caveat?

Dad (who is both tactless and desensitised to stories about cell-block hangings) joked that I could 'easily use a strip of the bedsheet' instead. 'In case you wanted any tips. I dunno what the first night's like. Depends what's on the telly ...'

Mum pulled a face, pinching, twizzling and breaking off the end of Dad's words with only a glare, abruptly terminating Dad's digression before he started ranking the items in the room I could use to kill myself.

I knew I was a drug addict. I never deluded myself into thinking otherwise. And right from the beginning, I didn't buy into the literary, romanticised notion of drug abuse – even the artful desolation of *Trainspotting*.

I was acquainted with the repetition and once-again-ness of addiction: procuring drugs > procuring drugs to achieve an ever-decreasing period of giddiness > > procuring drugs to achieve an ever-decreasing period of giddiness, followed by emptiness and existential reflection.

Sunday, 22 March 2015: I'd run out of dihydrocodeine tablets. Withdrawal was already kicking in, but 600 were being delivered to my flat, so I sat waiting – immobile, no television on, nothing – for hours and hours, in anticipation of their arrival. (As the limit was 200 tablets per purchase, and within a 30-day time-frame, I'd ordered from three different online pharmacies, lying through my teeth on the online questionnaires.)

I lived with my ex at the time – in the aforementioned shoe-box flat that smelled like mince – but she was at work. I had the 'freedom' to sit, for hours on end, with nothing but my thoughts. An extreme form of introspection. But when a delivery notification came through on my phone, I realised I'd accidentally ordered them to my old university address – in Portsmouth. Utterly frantic, and ignoring all other responsibilities (like meeting my girlfriend at the hospital where she worked, or buying our weekly shopping or paying our utility bills), I hopped on a train and did a round trip from Essex to Portsmouth just to get my fix.

On the way back, I turned off my phone to hide from my girlfriend, got high and watched a rabbi deliver a sermon about 'The Cosmic Tree with Divine Names' on my laptop.

That's drug addiction.

But the sitting and waiting for a thing that never arrives? That's also dementia.

Tom McCarthy, in an essay about Belgian writer Jean-Philippe Toussaint, writes about Toussaint's penchant for 'quasi-repeating narrative loops that see an eminently unreliable narrator trace and retrace circuits through corridors of a hotel' and his characters' 'obsessive attention to surfaces and objects'.

'The affect, here,' he continues, 'stems from the naïve individual's skewed encounter with systems larger than himself, an encounter which, reprised again and again, plays out Bergson's first rule of comedy: that life should be reshaped into a self-repeating mechanism.'

During my rehab induction with Napoleon (total respect for him – but ...), while the other assistants unscrewed the lids of my toiletries and poked in wooden sticks to check if I was smuggling drugs, I realised how residents must experience their first day in the care home. Like Larry in his hospital gown watching me rummaging through his bag.

I'm there itemising their meagre possessions. Strangers are bombarding them with false niceties. Family members (if they're lucky enough to have them*) nervously wring their hands – and a bloated black cloud hangs over the occasion. They can't quite pinpoint the source of this impending doom, this portentousness. But it's there. And from then on the resident is navigating their way through a bureaucratic maze without a map or a fully functioning mind – and forever bumping their head on an impenetrable glass partition.

At least I could eventually leave.

I see so many of the residents in this situation. I watch the strange actions – *mysterious* actions – of these confused and fretful people, but I don't have the record of their past experiences to make sense of their motivations. What I get is a jumble of fragments that we carers haven't got the time or the resources to assemble. (Though I'd *love* to reach back in time and touch the

---

* If they haven't got anyone to support them, in legal parlance this is called being 'unbefriended': 'At the time the decision must be made for someone who lacks the relevant capacity, that person is unbefriended if he or she has "no family or friends that it would be appropriate to consult" about the decision; that is, they "have no-one else (other than paid staff) to support or represent them or be consulted"' (from *Dementia, Law and Ethics: A Practical Guide for Nurses and Other Healthcare Professionals*).

hands of their past selves, to briefly penetrate their former coherence. To see Edith with hair and Arthur with legs.)

Hattie has been in the home for a while. I've seen her on days where reality reasserts itself and she sits staring at her feet for 14 straight hours, usually in the conservatory or her bedroom. No more gymnastics or chucking grenades from behind the drinks trolley.

She's at that awkward stage where she has too much of each way. Her sanity encroaches on her dementia and reminds her she doesn't belong here, but then – in a blissful unbecoming – she suddenly fits in again. Manically reciting nursery rhymes and riddles.

Still – we could all learn to be a bit more like Hattie (minus the periods of elective muteness, where she departs from the social realm). Formidable, extravagant Hattie. Stealing the sugar and chucking the 'dead' into the back garden, as if she were doing a bit of spring cleaning. I must have been working in care for too long because, in some ways, I actually think of her as an aspirational figure, a quixotic force of nature.

• • •

One of the many facets of opioid addiction is that it gives you a false sense of receptivity and openness. Back when I was getting high every day of the week, I was operating under the false belief that my brain was zoning in on missed details; on the novelistic potential of a normal, quotidian life. (Really, I was just experiencing reduced anxiety because opiates depress your central nervous system.*)

After initially achieving clarity-that's-not-really-clarity, and a few good months of balancing drug abuse with other areas of life, you eventually drift away, into the murk of opiate dependence.

Using sedatives, or even major tranquillisers, to subdue a resident or curb 'anti-social' and 'disruptive' behaviours used to be known in the trade as a 'chemical cosh'. And I've witnessed it plenty of times within the care home. A drastic change in a resident's demeanour after a visit from the GP, their agency eliminated as they're shuffled into a mental smog. Often the root cause of a resident's aggressive outburst, or any other 'malfunction' in their conduct, is down to their not being listened to, or a carer's rudeness towards them, or the expectation that they comply with directives set by a person they neither recognise nor trust. (This isn't always the case. With Barry, for instance, it's hard to determine what's triggered him.) The underlying reasons for undesirable behaviour should be examined before we resort to pharmacological solutions. But plying the residents with medication, and forcing them into a lobotomised half-life, is, to some managers, an expedient route to tranquillity – and in a job where

---

* They can also make you overfamiliar, forgetting that you can't send a picture of your socks, along with the message 'Look how well the stripe lines up with the bottom of my jeans', to a television producer you've only met once, and didn't even have a proper conversation with. (This ignorance of social conventions is also noticeable in people with dementia.)

staff are permanently burdened with a high workload, cutting corners is enticing.*

But errors in prescribing, monitoring, dispensing and administering medication in UK care homes are primarily caused by a few common recurring problems: a lack of communication between the home, practice and pharmacy; a lack of adequate medicines training among care staff; excessive drug-round interruptions; disorganisation, leading to inaccurate medicine reports or deficient ordering systems; and doctors who are unacquainted with the residents, inaccessible to the residents or disregard the information being passed on to them by care staff.

As I know from experience, being trapped in drug dependence – dazed and stupefied, barely able to speak – is a horrible state to be in. A spiritual negation. And for that reason, I struggle to see how facilitating a person's transition into stupefaction – and doing it without their express consent – is a form of care. I hate it. I hate to see people reduced to zombies all for the sake of convenience or as a result of errors that could easily be remedied – if, indeed, there was a willingness to be thorough when assessing an elderly person's care needs. I'd much rather deal with a pain in the arse than a ghost in perpetual surrender.

---

* In the past, to ensure that a manager's request for stronger medication is approved, carers have been asked to embellish or fabricate behavioural charts to support their request. The more examples of bad behaviour documented in a resident's personal file, the higher the chance of a doctor giving the green light to pharmacological intervention.

There are also plenty of other options outside of pharmaceutical intervention. For instance, regular physical activity and appropriate levels of stimulation. And these can be a lot more effective in managing restlessness and irritability than a cocktail of pills.

When I was in rehab, my therapists helpfully pointed out, during our daily group sessions (which were held in a small, homely room with a circle of padded armchairs), that, while I hadn't written anything for a year and hadn't gigged in five months, newly clean and in the Addiction Treatment Programme, I was producing extensive daily diaries.

They said they always looked forward to reading them – 'They're like novellas' – though one of my earliest CoGs (Change of Goals) was 'Don't over-intellectualise everything or use humour as a diversionary tactic.' These 'tics' could obstruct my ability to drill into my emotional core.

I was in these group therapy sessions with a guy named Jason – a white working-class archetype with a taut, muscular physique, tribal tattoos, impish grin, large jug ears and a gap between his front teeth. A steroidal Bash Street Kid. Even though he was in rehab, he still had this antic, coke-head energy that, more often than not, remained on the right side of rambunctious.

By the second day, we were blood brothers. That's what rehab does to you. Fast-track bonding. He was rowdy, over-sexualised and puerile. He had flare-ups of anger. Everything you'd expect. But he was also extremely vulnerable and needy and cried more than anyone else in the group. A teddy bear.*

As one of my therapists said while responding to these daily diaries, and encouraging me to tap into my baseline, 'All we want to know is if you're sad, hungry or horny.' Maybe they were looking for something akin to the stripped-back, functional entries in a resident's daily obs records:

> Today Arthur ate well/drank plenty of fluids. He's been assisted with all personal care, including washing, dressing and toileting.
>
> Regular catheter care given – though please refer to the behavioural chart re. 'catheter baptism'.
>
> He's regularly interacting with people, and participating in activities, but there's been occasional outbursts of anger or frustration.

But in the same way that medication can benumb the faculties of the person taking it, these records cast aside the fundamental

---

* On one excruciating occasion, Jason bowled over to a table in the dining room where the people with eating disorders were congregated – an especially charged time for them. And, with the best of intentions, he shouted, 'I know you lot worry about your weight and that but, honestly, I think you all look bangin'. You've got nothing to worry about.' He then turned to me and shouted, 'I bet you wish you had an eating disorder though, you fat cunt!' – followed by a big, rasping laugh as he patted my belly with the back of his hand.

character of the person they're documenting. They reduce them to a few basic actions or the vague murmurs of bodily desire and instinctive processes. And the same thing happens when the separate spheres of care work – the medical, the commercial and the therapeutic – aren't accorded equal importance. When paramedics are working against carers, or when carers are committing acts of civil disobedience (or minor property damage) to rankle directors. Urgent medical needs – meaning *bodily* needs – are prioritised. And knotty, intransigent mental health problems are shunted down to the bottom of the pile.

If we're to provide the best possible standard of care – one that opens the individual up like a paper chain, revealing the many layers of their personhood – our approach should encompass expressiveness and raw emotion, but also expert knowledge and pragmatism; it should be a mix of the functional and the dysfunctional – and embrace creativity and empathy to coincide with official evaluations, protocols and cognitive and clinical insights. It should be complex and involve many variables – unlike the 'guidance' that's issued from the headquarters of care provider corporations.

• • •

The header in my rehab diary reads 'ATP Daily Reflective Diary'. This is followed by a subheader: 'Please ensure that your completed diary is in one of the ATP post boxes in either Chelmer Ward or the Lodge by 8.30am.' I found the structure and routine of these daily diaries – and the timekeeping that was expected of us at the centre, including our punctuality at group sessions or therapeutic activities – to be beneficial. It's the once-again-ness, the thing that's so counter-productive in the midst of active addiction, but done right. Still, when does a routinised existence turn into institution-alisation? It's a question I constantly wrestle with when thinking about care work. What's in the residents' best interest? Routine has a stabilising effect, reduces agitation and helps to imprint new information, but what is a life without variety?

Underneath the headers there's a brief instruction: 'Use this form to share what has been significant for you in treatment over the last 24 hours. As a guide, try to express your FEELINGS as well as your thoughts about where YOU are presently on the programme and anything that you wish to share regarding your recovery.'

In her book *Notes Made while Falling*, Jenn Ashworth recounts her early years as a doctrinaire Mormon and the Mormon Church's tradition of record-keeping and journaling. According to Spencer W. Kimball, one of the religious leaders featured in Ashworth's book, 'Your own private journal should record the way you face up to challenges that beset you.' But success stories only, please: 'Personally I have little respect for anyone who delves into the ugly phases of the life he is portraying, whether it be his own or another's. The truth should be told, but we should not emphasise the negative. Even a long life full of inspiring experiences can be brought to the dust by one ugly story. Why dwell on that one ugly truth about someone whose life has been largely circumspect?'

I couldn't disagree with this more.

I think it's vital that we show the variegated chaos of human nature and not deprive readers – whether God or future children or you suckers – of a biography with the gristle left on.

In the care home, I wish we had the time to create an expansive record of the residents' daily lives. The temporary alliances. The little acts of vengeance. The polyphonic squabbles at a table full of elders, each of them having separate conversations, running in tandem though never combining. (Sometimes you'll think you've caught two of them engaging in a conversation – only to discover each is wrapped up in their own monologue, speaking *to* the other, but both independent of one another.) Even the prurient comments made by indecorous old men – comments that are either tolerated, rebuked or artfully circumvented by care staff. It's all part of a normal workday for us. And afterwards, the carers reconvene in the CTM's office and argue whether the 'old boys' – the residents who are tapping into an essential goat-man lecherousness – were always like that or whether it's the dementia talking.*

The main symptom of Alzheimer's is memory difficulties, but with frontal lobe dementia – the diagnosis my nan received, which

---

* I remember one gentleman, while lying in his bed, with *Songs of Praise* on the television, asked me whether he could 'have a tug' on my 'female willy'.

is a lot rarer – there can be a warping effect on the personality as those who are affected become inappropriate and disinhibited.

As the frontal lobe plays a central role in human sexual behaviours – mediating our social and emotional responses or initiating, and sustaining, certain behaviours – the interactions of those diagnosed with this type of dementia can become problematic due to their sexualised overtures, though the individual is often unaware of how inappropriate they're being.

Of course these situations can be challenging, but why deny the uncomfortable truths of a person's lived experience – especially if we have insights into the underlying reasons for their 'aberrant' sociality? But the daily observation records are a diplomatic erasure of the 'ugly phases of life'. And it's a shame because we're missing so much. These elders traipsing along care home corridors, or staggering across carpeted lounges, like rusted figures in an automaton clock, forever in search of female willies.

'Some people ... are abject because they are similarly expelled from the social body,' writes Philip Scepanski in an essay entitled 'Addiction, Abjection, and Humour: Craig Ferguson's Confessional Stand-Up'. 'This category applies generally to people at the margins of society including the homeless, mentally ill and addicts.'

A good example of the 'gristle'!

When people become symbolically connected to abjection, they're cut asunder and struggle to be fully integrated into the social body. But through confessing the 'ugly truth' – rebelling against the officialdom of social etiquette – we make the unpalatable parts of ourselves 'familiar'. And once they're familiar, they're on their way to being rehabilitated. Or if they're not totally accepted, at least we've deepened people's understanding of them.

This understanding, and acceptance, is one of the tent poles of holistic humanism. In his article 'Peripheral Proust', Adam Gopnik writes about a recurring theme in Marcel Proust's work, noting that the novelist regularly 'dramatized the relationship between cruelty and tenderness'. Likewise, the appetite for kindness and delicacy along with humiliation and savagery is a fundamental part of the dynamics within the care home.

Why do you think I gravitated towards care work? Because it's teeming with both compassion and conflict, with healthy personas and an oscillating morality. It's just *ripe* with humanity. Plus, I'm more at ease sitting with Arthur, reassuring him that the pressure he can feel is caused by a catheter balloon and he hasn't sucked up his bollock through his knob hole – I'm more comfortable in these marginal spaces, with (unfairly) marginalised people, than I am situated in the mainstream. That's why I'm not ploughing the same furrow as the hedonistic party boys of stand-up comedy. I got high and sought friendship in a care home, for Chrissake.

· · ·

It's 11.30am. We're beyond the mad morning rush – at least until we gear up again in preparation for lunchtime. It was a morning of squatting, hoisting and forgetting to lift with my legs. Tension in my shoulders and pain in the lower back. Turning, stripping, and dumping dirty laundry into red bags. Tubs full of food scraps and plates in the sink. I even introduced Larry to his new 'housemates' – before he promptly decided to turn around and return to his bedroom. (When Larry peered into the lounge, Arthur was interrogating a toy monkey and Barry was stamping on a clatter of imaginary tanks. Larry said, 'I think that'll be plenty, thank you,' and then walked away.) Hallmark Christmas films were still on the TV in the lounge because no one's changed the channel since the second week of December. Dorothy picked up a Connect Four counter and asked, 'Are these to eat?' – before Ligaya rushed in to stop her.

I took it upon myself to assign morning breaks. I asked Ligaya if she was happy to go first, and now it's my turn. Usually there's a tacit agreement between carers and their CTM (a one-sided agreement) that if we're short-staffed, we should forego our 15-minute breaks – but fuck that.

Outside it's still cold and drizzling. I'm sitting in the staffroom on a salmon-pink leatherette sofa with plump cushions. It's the first seat to be claimed if the staffroom is busy – but carers, if they can help it, will avoid working on New Year's Eve, so there's not many of us knocking about.

I'm reading through my rehab diary again, having retrieved it from the rucksack I slung on top of the staffroom lockers. (This is where I always leave it.) As my work life is tied to my using, I started bringing the diary in with me so I could dip into it whenever I felt a bit tweaky. A way of reminding myself of my triggers, my patterns of behaviour, etc. Ultimately, to remind myself to stay clean.

In the first entry, dated Friday, 3 February 2017, I wrote:

I've found the experience to be very cathartic so far. There was an automatic intimacy between me and the rest of the people in the ATP programme. I felt uninhibited enough to share my thought processes; complete disclosure. Sometimes my initial instinct is to withdraw, to become cloistered, but I was open to the group.

Physically, I've been agitated. And in between sessions it was difficult to achieve any psychic tranquillity. I read *The Lonely Man of Faith* by Joseph B. Soloveitchik but was distracted by news events. I even get a narcotic effect off of the news cycle and daily updates about Trump. Anything that will stimulate my brain.

There's been a few visual triggers today, e.g. a packet of dihydrocodeine in the pharmacy. Even the colour scheme of the packet is a trigger. Even the sound of the blister packs! (Though that's an aural trigger. Ears.) It reminds me of the ritual of drug abuse.

Though I'm slightly self-conscious, I'm using polished 'articulation' to masquerade true, raw emotion during group sessions. I want people to think I'm funny and a good orator.

On the back of the sheet, in a section entitled 'Fears', I put 'That I won't achieve anything. That when I die, I'll have no legacy and no children.'

The following day I obviously downgraded my priorities: 'Mild panic because I ran out of Mini Eggs. They've become a replacement drug. And now I've substituted Mini Eggs with chain-bathing (I keep having baths).'

Underneath, as part of my 'Gratitude List', I wrote, 'I'm grateful for the continuity and the structure of the weekly timetable.'

On Sunday, 5 February 2017, I'm a lot more addled and manic. The entry starts with an apology – 'Sorry about any extraneous details' – and unfurls into a nutty little essay that fluctuates between 'Da Vinci used to channel latent homosexuality into prolific workmanship' and 'I've replaced Mini Eggs and baths with apples. I wasted half an hour wrapping Sellotape around a can of Coke Zero for no reason whatsoever.'

I'm struck by the similarities between these futile, compulsive acts, fuelled by my own bewilderment, anxiety and agitation, and those of the residents I'm caring for, who incessantly knit without needles and yarn, or stamp on tiny tanks, or sit waiting to be activated by elusive guides who never appear.

As I'm reading, the cleaner that looks like an overgrown baby skulks into the staffroom. He's a sweet person – a harmless malingerer – but he has a habit of appearing at the exact moment you want to be left alone. And even though he has an equal right to occupy this space, he uses it so much – especially on days like today, when management isn't in.

There's another problem: his pathological shyness is made manifest with every awkward encroachment into your personal space, which is followed by his panicked retraction, and then a string of apologies. And people like this make my heart sore. They're so clearly ill at ease with themselves, and how they relate to other human beings, and I want to offer reassurance – but it would never subdue the unrest within. (I've been there. I know. I get it.)

And because of this constant nervousness, and social ineptitude, his very presence in the room becomes burdensome. You can't help but take on his emotional baggage. And, eventually, this curdles into an unexpressed exasperation. (We're breaking our backs caring for the elders; can't the staff sort themselves out?) Whenever he's around, and jittery, and eyeing me timidly as he pours a cup of coffee, I think, *You're a proper imposition.* (How horrible is that? To think about a person that way?)

'Is that … that … is that *The Da Vinci Code?*' he asks, with both a lisp and a stutter (double whammy!), pointing at my rehab diary. (It's a green ring binder containing hole-punched sheets of paper.)

'Ah, nah. It's just a thing I had to write when I was in hospital,' I reply, suppressing a desire to say *Of course it's not the fucking Da Vinci Code! It's a ring binder!*

I changed 'rehab' to 'hospital' to avoid the social stigma. (An unfair, retrograde view of drug treatment programmes – but one that still holds some sway in Conservative Essex.)

'I went to hospital. Or not hospital but … it was for my … I've got my … it was for my social anxiety. I'm really anxious all the time,' he replies.

I'm forced to weigh up my priorities in real time. Here's a person in pain looking to ignite the leaping sparks of friendship – sparks that jump between two people who have a shared experience, who have both been in institutions. Do I indulge my selfless, chivalric side and surrender to a delicacy of feeling, or do I opt for unrepentant self-interest?

I'm feeling tired and suddenly I don't have the energy for a stilted, going-nowhere conversation. And I want to think of a graceful, effortless way to step back and exit the situation.

'Sorry, I need a shit,' I reply. Then I stand up, tuck the ring binder under my armpit and go to the en suite attached to the staffroom.

· · ·

There's a man I care for, Ed, who regularly asks for updates on my comedy career.

Earlier this morning he asked, 'You got any of that Lee Evans money yet?'

I quickly changed the subject.

He's in his late seventies, totally bald, with faded tattoos like ink bleeding through toilet paper, and an entire body that looks like it's been nicotine-stained. His movements are fretful, dogged and sudden. Everything is done at a half-sprint. And like Ayaan, who went to the Diamond Centre, he seems to be perpetually tormented and restless – though eager to 'muck in' and to not cause any additional stress for the carers. He's always making tea for other residents or gathering used mugs, cups and saucers and loading them into the sink.

On such occasions, Tracy might bark, 'You actually gonna wash 'em?' while she's tapping away on her phone and sitting with her feet up on a stool she's taken from Evie. (Unfortunately, because of Tracy, I can't completely disabuse the stereotype of 'lazy carers'.)

For some reason Ed's found a sense of kinship with Ethel – with her infectious laugh and slightly garbled, country-fied accent, and blue hair that looks as if she dyed it using an HP ink cartridge. When he gives a few quid to a carer so they can fetch him 'proper biscuits' or sweets from the shop, he'll load half the treats onto a saucer and pass them to Ethel. She always accepts this kind offering without a single word exchanged.

Almost always the final two awake – 'left for the night staff' – they'll watch TV in the lounge and work their way through the treats, barely acknowledging each other's presence. Occasionally she might pat him on the hand and say, 'Thanks, Dad. Locking up the ol' goats tomorrow.'

It's 12.45pm. After checking on a few bed-bound residents – and those who remain in their rooms either due to choice or medical necessity (like if they have scabies, an infestation where mites implant eggs under the skin) – I return to the lounge to find Ligaya. She's stressed out, sweaty and has a halo of flyaway hairs surrounding her head.

'They all been stupid basta'ds, Pope. Flippin' heck, I tell you.'

'What's been going on?'

'They go cuckoo. I dunno what's been happening to them. They all go at once like this.'

'Ah, shall we start taking them into the dining room?'

'Yes, yes. Luckily Ed's been so helpful. And it's sweet with these two, you know?' Ligaya says, indicating Ed and Ethel. 'They're just friends but he looks after her. It's very nice to see it.'

The opposition of temperaments contained within me – within all of us, really – also resides in the residents and their complicated backstories. And as I keep banging the drum for best practice, including fleshing out the people you're caring for and avoiding the pitfalls of weak, sentimentalised representation, Ed is a good example of density within the nature of the self as he defies the 'kindly old man' characterisation. You snag on broken glass and rusted nails if you delve too deeply.

But it's normal to bounce between light and shade. Or, as in rehab, the swing from Jason's tears to my 'intellectualising' and joke-making. Or the constant fluctuations of cruelty and tenderness. But to focus on 'tenderness' for a moment.

This is the thing I love about the care home.

The tender little rituals that arise organically, without any instruction or forward planning behind them. Or the small acts of kindness and protection (like Ed sharing his sweets or springing up and rushing to the bathroom to get Ethel some tissues). And, from then on, they become embedded.* Part of a shared routine and a platonic 'relationship', of sorts.

Samuel Taylor Coleridge wrote in a notebook from 1796, 'Poetry – excites us to artificial feelings – makes us callous to real ones'. Even though the demands of care work, and the unreasonable conditions, can mummify your affections – you forget there's also very real, and very nourishing, communication there. A chemical plume of love and fondness. And – as care assistants – we regularly build on this human connection.

There's always been friction between medical and holistic support within care homes – with the former being prioritised over the latter. I'm here to improve a resident's well-being, and, even though I've gleaned only a surface knowledge of the medical and biological (it's good to keep blood *inside* the body), I observe interactions and responses to develop an intuitive understanding of the *person* rather than the *illness*. And by doing this, I avoid a doctor's habit of seeing 'people with dementia' as one homogenous group, and the cold and mechanistic approach of scientific reductionism.

On Twitter I had an argument with a biomedical practitioner when I wrote that – despite their vital, world-changing work in helping us 'understand what causes the pathology associated with

---

* I have my own mad rituals. I go jogging as the sun is setting, beside a motorway near my house – and the vanishing point at the end of the motorway happens to align perfectly with the setting sun. I try to complete the length of the motorway before the sun goes away. Basically, I'm trying to outrun the sun. That's one of them.

dementia [thus] advancing biochemical or biological knowledge' – their specialist role differs from that of support practitioners.

I wrote that there's a tendency for the biomedical perspective to dehumanise people. That's where I come in. If my work has *any* value (which, judging by my opponents' silence on this particular matter, she doesn't believe it does), it's the ability to balance this out.

The biomed practitioner made clear – having reiterated it in every reply, alongside my own praise of her profession – that she's doing a very impressive job. But as she also stated, 'biomed do not work with patients directly', and that her focus is on 'understanding … the diversity of diseases that cause dementia and different manifestations'. Which confirmed my point, really.

I know some of these doctors *hate* for their authority to be challenged by a lowly carer – even though I wasn't disputing anything being written – so I tried to sugar the pill: 'We could turn this into a David vs. Goliath thing where I'm the lowly carer (BTEC in Art & Design, son!) telling the greatest minds of the biomed community, "Nah, you're talking shit, mate. Dementia can be cured with raisins. I saw it in a dream. And that's science."'

But, still, she wasn't having any of it. And it ended with me writing: 'What you're doing is VITAL, IMPORTANT work. (Which is something I've said quite a few times now.) I'm not putting my job as a carer in the same league as the work you're doing. Realistically, it's nowhere near. But if there's one tiny bit of value that I may provide as a carer – AND THAT'S NOT

TREADING ON YOUR TOES, PROFESSOR! I'LL MAKE SURE
I END WITH MORE PRAISE! – if there's a tiny, tiny bit of value
I can provide, it's that I'm spending 70 hours a week with a resident and I might get to know them a bit better as a person. But,
yeah, you're doing good work.'

Basically I turned into a dickhead. And lied about doing 70
hours a week.

• • •

I rap on Ed's door frame to let him know lunch is ready and to
ask if he'd like to come down to the dining room. (His bedroom
is only two doors along from it, opposite the staff toilet and the
supply cupboard full of pads, gloves, lining and so on.)

After escorting Ethel to the dining room, and pulling out her
chair to assist her with sitting down, he returned to his room to
get some money. (I told him he wouldn't need it and that meals
are included in the overall fee for residential care, but he went to
get it anyway.)

He's perched on the edge of his mattress, jiggling his legs and
percolating with nervous energy. He's in the middle of an elaborate conversation with himself ('I'm always the middle man but
the middle man's not me') and making roll-ups that *should* last
him until tomorrow – but rarely do.

I poke my head around the partially open door.

'Eddy Eddy Eddy!' I shout, unable to gauge how loud I'm being.
'You alright? Do you wanna come down to the dining room?'

'That's a bit mad, isn't it?' he replies, a half-smile on his face. 'Talking to yourself. I'm a bit mad for doing that, aren't I?'

'Honestly – don't worry about it, Ed,' I reassure him. 'Sometimes this place can send you a bit bloody crazy, y'know. I start muttering to myself as well. But if you're bored, and feeling a bit agitated, you know you can always come and chat to me. It'll never be an imposition.'

The last time he took me up on this offer, he told these baroque, barely concealed lies. (Actually, they're more 'tall tales' than lies.)

I was sitting in the lounge, filling out some charts, and suddenly he stormed into the room and plonked himself in the chair beside me. Without any segue, and in his breathless, unpunctuated delivery, he said, 'I worked for the Queen and defused a bomb I found in her Mercedes and it was planted there by the IRA and Saddam Hussein.'

'Ah, that's mad, Ed. You've actually had quite a storied life,' I replied, playing along.

'And I killed them all and drove them to the Isle of Wight and threw them off the cliff but I got a Purple Heart for that so it ended up being a nice day out all told. Anyway, I'll have my sandwiches in my room.'

Then – as quickly as he arrived – he was gone again.

But, according to various assessments, Ed has capacity. He even handles his own finances. In our dealings with him, we're always straddling a fine line between respecting his autonomy and preserving his health and well-being. That tension is part of the job. For instance, he often refuses to wash or change his clothes, but all we can do is encourage him. Or – unofficially – incentivise washing and dressing.

He arrived as one of the 'unbefriended', flanked by harried social workers brandishing folders full of documentation. One with glasses and flyaway hairs sticking out of a sagging bun; the other with a short, sharp hairstyle and mauve lipstick.

'Lesbians,' Ed said to me on the first day, after they'd left, 'or sisters. Not that I've got a problem with either.'

Pat – a reliable source of gossip – passed on some scandalous details that had been provided by a toothless neighbour, with dirt under his yellowing nails, who sometimes came to visit: he'd held his wife hostage with a whaling harpoon he'd bought from an antique dealer; he was a drunk; he was a 'wrong 'un'.

'Keep an eye on 'im. But if he tries it with me, I'm locking him inside the medicine trolley,' she said.

'What if he's got a whaling harpoon?' I replied.

'Key between the knuckles.'

'Yeah, I'm sure that'll withstand a whaling harpoon, Pat.'

Tolerance, mercy, generosity, intelligent kindness – these are the attributes of a good carer. It's about accepting individuals as they come and leaning in to the utter ordeal of 'people'. Knowing people. Chatting to people. Mourning people. Managing people. Succumbing to a vast mycelial network of sprouting emotion, personal entanglement and cumulative trauma. Of catastrophes and frustrations. Of jealousy, envy and vengefulness.

The two arenas where I've developed tolerance, or cultivated that merciful vision, are working in care and attending Narcotics Anonymous meetings.

Of course, there are behaviours that I don't condone – and I still believe there should be an injunction on harmful words and actions, or the repercussions to such words/actions – but I'm conditioned to accept the unstable boundaries of the self. And in devoting a chunk of my adult life to patient-centred health care, and recognising both the differences and similarities in other people's values, interests and capabilities, I've stretched my moral responsibilities to include entire communities – or the 'common self'. And part of a good communitarian health-centric approach is holding your hands up and saying, 'Some people will point a harpoon at their loved ones. C'est la vie! Peoples be peoples, ay.'*

Back in 2020 I was trading DMs with another comedian, engaging in a back-and-forth about cancel culture. Even though it's become a nebulous, imprecise concept – a wall for people to project their own anxieties onto – it isn't a totally baseless phenomenon. Most people spend their lives online now. It's there that I've noticed a diminution of socially sanctioned behaviour. And the more abbreviated the list of acceptable conduct becomes, the

---

* I'm being flippant for comic effect. Domestic violence is no joke. But part of accountability is the opportunity for a person to explain themselves – and Ed is no longer a reliable narrator. And what good would ostracising, penalising or punishing a confused old man do? Though his family would have every right to harbour such animosity. That's family stuff. It's always complicated.

more ruthless and exacting we are in our moral determinations. This ends up being at odds with the care ethics we're supposed to uphold.

We're regularly confronted with the evident fallibility of man. The transgressions, the misdeeds, and then those who are *truly* guilty and dangerous.

But it's all part of the carer's repertoire: clearing a path towards forgiveness and redemption – with some heavy lifting from the transgressor – and using grace to counter wicked impulses (in you or someone else). And like doctors, who can't discriminate against the person in need, we have to take on these elders and accept the broken glass and rusted nails.*

The meat of an NA meeting is a series of auricular confessions, minus the attendant absolution. And sometimes the people in these meetings are holding their hands up to truly despicable acts. (It's against the spirit of the thing to reveal specifics, but domestic abuse is a common offence.†)

---

* The fact I made a false equivalence between care workers and doctors, and their respective occupational worth, is going to piss off a lot of doctors. And to any doctors reading this (especially if they're middle-aged men) I say: I could do your job. I could do it with my eyes closed. (1) Keep the blood inside the body. (2) Don't compare another human being to a worm. 3) When you're murdering patients with a syringe driver, refer to it as 'managing symptoms' rather than 'euthanasia'.

† There can also be harmless confessions. I once admitted to participating in cannibalism sex chat. Standard dom/sub shit. It was initiated by the woman I was seeing and I didn't really get it. I sent her a text that read 'I'm going to swallow your boobs'. Nothing else. She followed up with 'Maybe this isn't your thing'.

I instinctively recoil when hearing such revelations. *I thought this geezer was alright!* But we're in a town hall or repurposed gymnasium, holding on to cups of lukewarm tea and sacrificing an evening watching Netflix, as a necessary step towards redemption. Actually, towards more than redemption; the purpose of confessing is to open oneself to, in Marilynne Robinson's words, 'something purer and grander than mercy, something that puts aside the consciousness of fault, the residue of judgement that makes mercy a lesser thing than grace'.

In my capacity as a carer, I've scanned the communal areas of the care home and asked myself, *How many of these old men have beaten their wives? How many of these frail and shrunken people have ostracised black neighbours or spat racist abuse at new arrivals?*

It's a dark thought – but they're a product of an era when young men returned from war as stammering, traumatised souls (at least internally), and people in general were unable to summon the language of psychic disturbance. Or a time in which majoritarian whiteness was wrongly seen as a form of manifest destiny and the civil rights revolution hadn't yet addressed race relations in the UK.

Who's to know? These details are scrubbed from the potted biography we're given by family members. And I tend not to lead with 'Is Dad a vehement racist?' (If he is, then his old knob will *not* be getting washed. At least not to the exacting standard I'm known for.)

Old knobs aside, I hope that with each subsequent generation the harm of what came before will be burned off like sulphur impurities. But – on an individual level, on a *cellular* level – the effects of ageing diminish a person and whatever evil has been committed by them in the past; it'd be like squaring up to a mushroom to confront it now.

There's always a path to salvation. And even if someone gets to a point where they're old and decrepit and still haven't taken it, they're going to discover a new-found innocence in senility, be cared for by African, Eastern European and Filipino workers, and – most likely – die under strip lighting with only me for company. Me, sitting by their bed, moistening their lips with a glycerine swab, talking about how I've run out of Mini Eggs or the time I got an acorn stuck in my belly button. Imagine that. My face being the last face you ever see. *That's* when justice is restored.*

• • •

It's now night-time – 8.15pm – at the care home. We've been jammed up with the usual mistakes, near misses and medical errors – whether it's an unsupervised resident trying to stand on their own, and being caught *just* in time by a passing carer, or someone vomiting after breathing in too much deodorant in

---

* I've watched approximately ten people die. With one old man, I rested my copy of the *London Review of Books* on his blanketed legs while I read it. (I asked him first. He was fine with it. But using a dying man as a lectern – it's a bit morally perilous, isn't it. Though, as someone said on Twitter, 'You could think of it as a measure of friendliness that had developed'. I love that. That's the point I want to get to with my elders: being comfortable enough to use them as a work surface.)

a small, unventilated space, or a skin tear caused by a distracted carer during a pad change.

We're legally obligated to report and record injuries, diseases and dangerous occurrences as part of RIDDOR (Reporting of Injuries, Diseases and Dangerous Occurrences Regulations) 2013. In theory, this should help to mitigate risks, or the chances of sickness and infection, but manually logging an incident in the accident book only becomes a priority if (1) someone is in immediate danger (losing blood, has a communicable disease, drank something poisonous, had a fall, etc.) or (2) there's a chance of legal blowback. So near misses aren't recorded and can't be analysed for patterns of problematic or hazardous behaviour.

Is a resident attempting to walk because they're restless and agitated? If so, what preceded the incident where this resident nearly fell? If you nearly hit a resident's shin with a wheelchair's foot plate, what frame of mind were you in? What were the underlying reasons for this absent-mindedness? Were you trying to remember too many things at once? Without answers to these questions, the glitches within the system continue to be overlooked, and no one is paying attention to big-picture improvements – or the incremental tweaks that make up systemic change. Every now and again, I'll be motivated to write a report, or a recommendation, that might lead to the implementation of new ideas within the care home – but then I think, *Nah.*

As far as I can tell, most of the problems are down to critical staff shortages anyway. That or miscommunication (or noncommunication), a manic work rate, poor record-keeping and no concrete procedures for conflict resolution, but a lot of these derive from the original sin of 'no fucking staff'.

Either way, the mania of the previous 13 hours dries up, and is forgotten, during this final stretch of the shift; this comedown.

Every other resident is in bed except for Ed. He's making his sixth cup of coffee and is spilling granules with an unsteady hand.

It's the first time I've sat down – *properly* sat down – since the break at 11.30am. Earlier, I collected my rucksack from the staffroom and brought it to the lounge so I can leave through the conservatory door at 9pm, the end of the shift.

For the residents' safety, the conservatory door can only be opened by a little key attached to a chain on the inside wall. It's a complicated mechanism – not just a basic lock – so they're unable to operate it. Whenever I'm leaving, I reach in through a small window and strain to grab the key and lock the door from the inside. (As I'm doing this, any residents in the lounge look on, completely unperturbed.) Then I cut through the garden, past the bike rack and the shit bins and into the car park.

The NYE fireworks have already started, but nothing is happening indoors except for a slight raucousness on the live TV broadcast. Ed and I sit in quiet solidarity. The green binder is balanced on my knee. The 'buzzer' – or central alarm system – is going off, as it usually is. But I've already looked at the panel on the wall. It's an alert from a room upstairs. Occasionally I glance across the room, out of the conservatory windows, to see the silhouettes of congregated carers, with their cigarette cherries hovering like fireflies. When a firework goes off, they're briefly splashed with colour.

I rarely join them during fag breaks because (a) I don't smoke, and (b) they only want to talk about how good or bad local restaurants are. ('It's Nepalese. Is that, like, snakes and shit?') I can indulge in the Protestant work ethic – the pragmatism, realism and steadiness of purpose you often find in the care professions – but I can't abide the small talk. The parking, the 'lovely mint sauce', the meal deals, the potholes on Longdrive Avenue. The pennies of conversation. And if you try to broaden the pothole chit-chat to include discourse on public enterprise or radical local democracy, they'll say – well, Tracy says – 'I dunno about all that bollocks.'

One of my ex-girlfriends hated all the stuff I was into and ripped the shit out of me when, in an offhand comment, I said I had a 'rich interior life'. (She did as well – but she'd also talk for 45 minutes about her favourite time using a Groupon voucher.*) Plus, Dad, a self-declared anti-elitist, always holds me to account if I'm getting 'too poncy', too ideas-above-my-station.

Is an overly keen interest in current affairs elitist? And, as a carer, is it ill-suited? I've been disillusioned by the job for a while now, but a sense of loyalty to the people I care for has prevented me from leaving. Part of it is how much we're looked down upon

---

* I actually didn't mind those chats. I look back on them with a certain amount of fondness. Sometimes you need to be grounded by Groupon vouchers.

as carers; how low our social standing is. (Even though it's a completely unjust assessment, this is doubly true for the migrant workers who take these jobs, and work their arses off, and pay their taxes, but are still disaffiliated from the body politic in numerous different ways.)

Though in *Elitism: A Progressive Defence*, Eliane Glaser notes that, in the eighteenth century, 'the question of what makes something beautiful was the subject of lively public debate. Philosophers, poets and writers grabbed with both hands the task of defining beauty – and truth, for that matter – and their conclusions were picked over by a surprisingly engaged public.'

She goes on to declare that it's

time for progressives to free themselves of the muddle they have got into about 'elitism' [and] bring together the values of egalitarianism and intellectualism … We could rein back bureaucracy in public institutions and sweep away the empty and implacable demands on public bodies to be 'accountable to the public purse'. We could trust professionals, academics and artists to get on with what they want to do, rather than making them waste time on inefficient performances of public value – all those grant-bidding and form-filling and 'quality and standards' rituals.

Egalitarianism and intellectualism. Both these things represent an inner conflict. Within the context of care work – and life in general, to be honest – I've preached the benefits of cooperation, mutual aid and negotiation of the rules of living together. I've also asked for bureaucracy and form-filling to be scaled back; for the bushels of 'official documentation' to be set ablaze. I can be wankiness *and* the working man. But is there a way to successfully reconcile these two – both in me, the individual, and in society at large?

I don't know.

All I do is wipe arseholes for a living and then tell people about it onstage.

I'm not really supposed to have 'ideas'. And that's the same judgement I make against Tracy, etc. I'm just as guilty. But if we moved forward with this new 'progressive' elitism, choosing to collapse layers of bureaucracy and entrust 'professionals' with entire industries, who would be the primary candidates? It wouldn't be me. It wouldn't be Tracy. The same way I'm not even consulted when a decision must be made about a resident's day-to-day care needs. (Even though I'm the person who now spends more time with them than anybody else.)

I may have adorned myself with the epaulettes of an education (University of Portsmouth, no mucking about), but to a lot of people – to *most* people, especially that biomed practitioner – I'm a care assistant because I ran out of choices.* But we shouldn't discard or diminish the expertise of people in 'lowly'

---

* I've jumped to the same conclusions! But with Tracy – well, she really is only doing it because she ran out of choices. I judged that one correctly. She eats cheese strings for dinner. She's fucked.

jobs, in labour roles that have been *terminally* devalued with each subsequent generation. Because if people in high-up places actually consulted them, and invited them to the table, maybe we wouldn't see such a drastic withdrawal of state provision.

. . .

Ed is wearing a polo shirt covered in coffee stains of differing shades. Throughout the day I've asked him to change it and he keeps saying he'll do it later *or* that he's done it but re-spilt coffee in exactly the same place, leaving a stain identical to the one before.

'Ed, if you have a quick wash and change into a clean T-shirt for bed, I promise I'll take you out for a fag.'

Suddenly alert and straightening his posture – a dog that's just heard the word 'walkies' – he asks, with his machine-gun delivery, 'We're going now, are we? We're going for a fag now? I'll 'ave a wash and change and then we're going straight for a fag, yeah?'

'Yeah, but you have to get sorted first.'

'I'll get sorted, I can do that right now, I'll do it right now and then out for a fag, yeah?'

'Yeah.'

He then rushes out of the lounge, still holding a spoon full of coffee granules. (When he's this excited, he leads with his torso, stumbling forwards, as if he's in a race with his own feet.)

After about 10 minutes, he re-emerges wearing a *Family Guy* T-shirt (donated by one of the social workers?), a cardigan and stained jogging bottoms with an unnecessary brown belt tied around his waist. He always sleeps in his day clothes, never changing into pyjamas.

As I'm removing the belt, I look up and notice he's had a bit of a shave. It's a decent attempt, but there's some shaving cream on his neck. Plus, he's missed a few tufts of hair; his jawline looks like a scalped lawn with over-fertilised yellow patches. The landscape of his face has lumps and nodules – the sprouts that come with the pota-to'ing of age – but he's also retained the dimples and apple cheeks of his youth. And there's a boyish eagerness to him, accentuated by the newly revealed dimples, as he awaits feedback on his shaving.

'Looking pretty sharp, Ed!' I say. 'Missed a few bits but you can—'

'Yeah, I'll do it straight after but we're going for a fag now, yeah? I'm gagging for a fag.'

'Yeah, we're off.'

I try to wipe the shaving cream off his neck, but he's already moving towards the conservatory door that leads to the garden.

'There he is, that handsome boy,' says Ligaya, her voice float-ing through the dark.

'Oi, oi, hot stuff!' shouts Tracy. 'Wanna sit on my lap, Ed?'

Her laugh is punctuated by a little piggy grunt.

'Ligaya, did you hear what I—'

'Yes, I heard, Tracy,' says Ligaya, sombre-faced.

At 2pm – the start of the late shift – Ligaya had to switch sides and go to Harmony, because I'm a 'strong carer' who could pick up the slack of an underperforming partner. That's why the latest new girl has been dumped on me. (She's young, pleasant; will be gone in a couple of weeks.) Having worked with Tracy since then, Ligaya's reached her daily threshold.

'Going in now, so you three can have your little party,' says Tracy as she stubs out her cigarette and departs through the laundry room door.

I pass Ed his tobacco pouch, full of ready-made roll-ups and a lighter. When he lights one up and draws on it, it's as if he's trying to suck it out of existence with one protracted inhalation. The paper turns to ash like the flaking trunk of a silver birch.

'Ay, ay, ay. No more Tracy tomorrow, please,' groans Ligaya. 'She's telling me about her thrush and the sweat under her titties. The families come in and she's saying she's not bothered no more! She don't wanna do no more work!'

In exasperation, Ligaya presses her palm to her forehead.

'Remember the daughter that worked here?' she continues. 'The big, dumb – sorry, I don't mean to be … the big, dumb idiot. No wonder, you know? No wonder.'

Ligaya takes a couple more drags on her cigarette, looking wistfully at the sun receding into the horizon. She then stubs it out and drops it into the bucket of sand by her feet.

'Four more years of this. That's it. Then I'm done and going back home. I can't do much more. I'm an *old* lady now,' she says, then laughs the remaining frustration out of her system. 'I have to go and put the final ones to bed. That *fuckin'* buzzer still going as well. Goodnight, gents.'

I only manage a 'Nrrrr …' in return. (It's nice to know some-one long enough that it doesn't matter if I'm a rude prick.)

There's a pause – soon followed by the sound of seagulls, the trickle of the fountain, and the muffled clamour of the buzzer coming from inside the building. Barry, out of bed, stares at us through his bedroom window. He taps on the glass with his fingertips, mouths 'Enoch Powell' then lingers for a moment before closing his curtains.

'Night,' says Ed, a delayed response. One of many signs that he isn't as compos mentis as the doctors claim he is. Or had he clocked Barry in his vest and pyjama bottoms? The uneven drawstring with a knot in the end, swinging side to side like a pendulum. Maybe he'd seen him tapping the pane with his fluttering fingers, and Ed's farewell was directed at Barry, not Ligaya. Misunderstandings or miscommunication can often lead to false assertions being made about a resident's capacity. A rejoinder to a phrase or action that's been overlooked by a member of staff. A joke or a bit of irony, once rewarded in social circles, now seen as the ramblings of a half-wit.

We sit in comfortable silence as he sparks up another fag – the last one barely extinguished.

Addicts are brilliant at spotting one another. The insatiability. The restlessness. The interpersonal termination once a need has been met. Maybe that's why I'm both haunted by Ed and see it as my duty to be a surrogate son or nephew to him. I don't know. Maybe the *cared for* and *caregiver* dynamic has its own particular intimacies and doesn't need a comparison.

After the salty, shitty, strenuous labour of – I hate to phrase it like this – herding and manoeuvring human bodies (there's obviously a lot more to it, but that's the physical side), the respite is what I imagine the terminal calm of drowning to be like: the rest of the world slipping by overhead.

'I'm glad it's you bringing me out here. Some of the others don't speak,' says Ed, in a calm, unhurried manner, out of character for him. 'You're a good man, you are.'

'Ah, you're a good bloke as well, aren't you,' I respond, in a way that's more searching than I anticipated, hoping to scan his speech for remnants of his old harpoon-happy self, to listen for inflections that suggest latent remorse.

To my surprise, there's a trickle. A hint.

Something breaks free.

'My family never come to see me,' he says, his voice catching at the back of his throat.

The alarm ceases from inside the building. Someone – probably Ligaya – must have answered the buzzer.

It's the first time I've heard Ed say anything about a family. Is it children? Is he still married to the wife? They're obviously estranged.

'Families are weird, Ed. A lot of buried stuff. And you assume it'll get resolved, and time will do its job, but it can stay lodged in there, you know?'

I pride myself with having astute moral purchase and a great sympathy for Ed. But what do I owe his family?

To us carers, these elders might arrive as kindly, twinkly-eyed recumbents, and we're fond of them. They cause no bother. They may even lighten the workload if they're especially undemanding and agreeable (like Ed).

But when they die, and the children come to gather their paltry possessions, one of them might suddenly feel emboldened to speak candidly.

They pull you aside, away from the siblings, and give this unexpurgated assessment of the recently departed's parenting.

'Growing up, he made my life hell. I've never forgiven him for it. So fuck his fucking fishing trophy. Bin it. But don't let my sister catch you doing it.'

And thus concludes my supporting role in this family's 40-year melodrama.

On other occasions, the opposite can happen: a virtuous life is capped off by a few years as an arsehole with dementia. Let them have it! Perhaps it's weirdly liberating to smash your way through social situations minus the guard rails of politesse – and behind the aegis of diminished responsibility. That's the way to do it. Treat people well and save your selfish years for the end.

'Yeah,' Ed says, melancholia suspended in the air like vapour.

'Have you got a dad?' he suddenly asks. A few involuntary spasms ripple through his body.

It seems like an odd question.

'Yeah. He used to be a detective. Teacher now,' I reply.

'Do you love your dad?'

'Yeah. Yes. Like any father-and-son relationship, it has its moments, but, yeah, I proper love my dad.'

'I haven't drunk in months,' he says, apropos of nothing.

'That's really good, Ed. Do you feel better for it?'

'No. I feel worse for it. I 'ave nothing to wake up for.'

'Ah, Ed,' I reply, feeling gutted for him. 'You've got stuff going on. You've got ...'

I don't know how to finish that sentence.

'My dad,' I continue, 'once got attacked in the garden by a homing pigeon. I still remember seeing it through the window. Swooped down and dug its claws into Dad's head. I was only little. It was proper funny.'

Ed smiles – but in the give-and-take of conversation, I feel I owe him more for his vulnerability.

'But you know, my dad struggled to understand my addiction. Like, me being a drug addict. The son of a policeman,' I say.

Ed stops jiggling his knees and turns towards me.

'You? You're a drug addict?'

I never share this part of my life with residents, or their family members, in case the old stigma hasn't subsided as much as I thought. And I don't want to put myself in a situation where I notice their expression change as any goodwill that's been generated over the years drains away. *I thought this geezer was alright!* Then they start to worry they've been duped, that I'm not a safe pair of hands. Or that I'm stealing from their mum or cow-tipping their dad. (One of my proudest moments was when a family member secretly listened through the door, without my knowledge, while I assisted their grandad. And then – having owned up to this eavesdropping – said they were thrilled with how gentle and considerate I was. Thank God I did all my muggings in the morning that day!)

'Yeah,' I reply. 'My other job. Comedian, care worker, drug addict.'

'You don't seem like the type.'

'I suppose that highlights the universality of an addictive tendency.' (A pre-rehearsed line. I've said this a lot.)

'But you don't seem like a druggie.'

'Ah, that's probably good, innit.'

It's cathartic to say this to one of the residents. In the same way people with dementia can be homogenised, it happens to carers as well. It's assumed that we're all lazy, skeevy abusers. That's the media representation anyway. And saying 'I'm a drug addict' probably isn't the best way to counteract this stereotype (as addicts are often portrayed as lying, cheating scumbags with verrucas on their lips), but – if nothing else – Ed's actually *seeing* me. And as any comedian (who *all* have a crazed desire to maximise their visibility) will tell you: it's good to be seen.

'My Caffè Nero card,' says Ed, a stern expression overwhelming his face.

'What's that?

'Have you ever heard of the Caffè Nero coffee house?'

It is technically a house of coffee, but it's weird calling it that.

'Yeah. Is there one on the high street?' I ask, picking up this conversational thread.

'Yeah. And I had a card in my wallet where they put a thing on it, and if there's eight things I get a free coffee.'

'Like a loyalty card?'

'Yeah.'

'Ah, why don't you ask one of the carers to claim it for you?'

'I would – but the card went missing. It went missing from my wallet.'

'Ah, that's really shit, Ed,' I reply.

Ed pauses for dramatic effect, then turns to me and says, 'I won't be mad, but I'm just going to ask you once: did you steal my Caffè Nero loyalty card to buy drugs?'

And as with a lot of care home 'bonding', it's soon destabilised by the wheels coming off the conversation.

CHAPTER SEVEN

It's a crisp winter morning a few days after New Year's Eve. The vivid light made the walk from my house to the bus stop, just outside Southend Victoria train station, an unexpected pleasure.

I needed it. I needed some uplift because, lately, I've been ground down by life's circularity and the burden of responsibility, by the indistinct boundary between my work and personal life. If I'm not working, or gigging, I'll be at home. And when I'm at home I'll catch myself sitting in the lounge, doing nothing, or committing to futile activities like wrapping plumbing tape around an empty Coke can. (The reason? No reason. No reason whatsoever.) And I'll be wearing my home attire: a vest with a Bolognese stain on it and long johns that droop around the arse so that I look like a toddler with a full nappy. In those moments, I'm reminded that the elders and I are the same. Both of our worlds are small and constricted and by travelling from home to work, then work back to home, all I'm doing is hopping from one shoebox to another.* But it'd be a lot more bearable – having my energy depleted by 14-hour shifts or toggling between laborious- ness and inertia – if it came with respect, financial compensation or anything else that might enhance my self-esteem. (At least I have my Coke can wrapped in plumbing tape.)

'Labor, after all, is *us*,' writes Sarah Jaffe in *Work Won't Love You Back*. 'Messy, desiring, hungry, lonely, angry, frustrated human beings. We may be free to quit our jobs and find ones that we like better, as the mantra goes, but in practice that freedom is constrained by our need to eat, to have someplace to sleep, to have health care.'

In the care home you're expected to maintain a sunny dispo- sition. But conveying happiness and enthusiasm can be difficult when you're going through something. Whether that's feeling adrift, or the manic pulse that precedes a mental breakdown, it's hard to disguise it with fraudulent emotion. If you're suffering, the last thing you want to be doing is mashing up a kidney bean

---

* Social lives that lack vitality seem to be common among carers.

bolus (a lump of undigested food) inside a stoma bag to enable safe passage for shit.*

In a short story by Mavis Gallant titled 'The Burgundy Weekend', one of the characters says: 'Certain categories of people seem to be expected to laugh at their work.' By this they mean the help. The maids. The carers. With their hands 'chapped and covered with blood', but unable to rinse them 'so as not to bloody the clothes', all the while giving a 'gap-toothed and reassuring smile'. And the purpose of the smile, or forced laughter, is to ensure 'that the male guest[s] would not feel uneasy among women's disagreements'. This was written in 1971, a period when gender disparities were a lot more pronounced, but it still contains pertinent truths about care work, or domestic work, and how those employed in these roles are expected to present a sanitised public image. And how fucking exhausting it is to keep up that pretence.

My onstage persona has been described as 'cheeky yet in pain' – but, at the moment, I'm sick of grinning and bearing it. I don't want to 'yuk yuk' it up. For years I've been on 200 mg of sertraline per day, but this new wave of debilitating despondency is circumstantial. And the primary thing that's causing it is this: a deep dissatisfaction with the job I'm in. As my mum would say, 'I'm fed up to the back teeth with it.'

---

* A good metaphor for life, actually. Except the 'kidney bean bolus' represents my hopes and dreams.

Having knocked drugs on the head and experienced the benefits of sobriety, the final thing that's holding me back is doing a job that's devalued by almost every part of society. And, of course, it shouldn't be like this. We shouldn't live in a society where professional carers are ground down, where such a noble occupation starts to feel like a hindrance.

I say this kind of shit to shake people out of complacency and rouse them to action. Maybe it'll have an impact? Maybe it'll inspire them to defend minimum-wage employees, or encourage minimum-wage employees to demand better treatment? Having said this, I once delivered a similar pep talk to workers taking part in an online picket – and realised I was in the same Bolognese'y vest, the same ill-fitting long johns, and had a bowl of morning ice cream balanced on my lap (which I frantically ate before my dad woke up and shamed me for eating ice cream for breakfast). I'm not exactly a role model.*

The number 3 bus arrives at the stop and I set off towards the care home. I notice the homeless guy outside Marks & Spencer, sitting on a mound of dirty sleeping bags. We talk about Brexit. He offers up some of his theories. ('All politicians are gay.' And that was it. He left it there.) We eat the almond croissants I got us from the food hall. I then vocalise something that, up until now, has remained a vague intention.

'I'm quitting my job,' I say.

---

* Though because of the weight gain, and the breakfast ice cream, I'd make a decent roll model.

It's been at the back of my mind for a few months now, but after the wobble with Larry's drug bag, and the continued staff shortages, and the occupational burnout – the temptation to quit has taken on a new sense of urgency. I didn't realise how much until this conversation.

'You don't need it, man. Needing a job is a myth,' he replies.

'Yeah. Maybe.'

'Trust me. It's a myth. It's all lies. You don't need a job to live,' he says, fluttering his fingers towards a can of Red Bull sunk into one of the dirty sleeping bags. 'I've got what I need.'

There's a comfortable silence. The only people around this early in the morning are a few migrant nurses waiting at the bus stop.

'Remember wrestling?' he asks, changing the subject. 'Apparently that wrestler crippler crossfaced his son to death.'

'Ah, now *that's* a myth! He killed his son but—'

'Nah. It's not a myth. I've seen the video. Swear down.'

There's a pause.

'The son had braces,' he adds. A redundant detail he believes will sell the lie.

'Quality,' I say, brushing pastry flakes off of my Lyndon B. Johnson hoody. 'I better shoot off now. Keep safe. Look after yourself.'

* * *

It's now 9.45am and we're approaching the back end of the morning rush. I'm standing in the dining room, by the countertop next to the sink, preparing a second – or third – slice of toast* for any resident who wants one.

Susan W. keeps forgetting she's eaten, so I provide a rundown – 'You did well, Susan! Ate like a trooper!' – but she laughs (unable to figure out what, exactly, the 'joke' is) and waits for me to bring her some more. (There are days where she'll get angry as, to her, it's as if we're purposely missing her out – even if, like today, she's eaten.)

The majority of them have eaten well, having worked through tea and toast, followed by tea and cornflakes or a cooked breakfast (a small pile of scrambled egg, a tomato and a tangle of bacon that was mostly rind), or both. Some even opted for a yogurt as well.

Edgar is jabbing his walking stick at Arthur, who, throughout breakfast, wheeled himself from table to table, sidled up to other residents and accused them of various transgressions. (I overheard Arthur arraign Edgar for 'filling my birdhouse with blood'.)

---

* I get satisfaction from refining menial tasks, and incorporating them into a cooperative workflow, to enhance our collective productivity. (I know. I've got fuck all else going on.) For instance, finding a way to butter large quantities of toast that reduces mess and takes half the time. And, cumulatively, all these time-saving adjustments (whether it's a fluidity of motion or an uncluttered workspace) can have a profound effect on the smooth running of a shift. And when a shift is running smoothly, it improves the well-being of staff and residents. That's why I prefer working with Ligaya (who is gentle, while still being systematic and organised) as opposed to Tracy (who once washed a resident by squeezing a bottle of Buxton over his naked body. And when confronted, she responded, 'It's all water! What's the difference?')

'Get out of my eyeline, please,' says Edgar, quiet but firm, 'or I'll take away your arms as well.'

Arthur lets out a pompous, scenery-chewing laugh, and punctuates it with a line that – to him – must be a sting in the tail, a wicked bon mot:

'Joke's on you because my arms are cannons!' he shouts, holding up two normal arms.

'You're a bloody nutcase,' says Edgar, before standing up, staggering out of the dining room and making his way down the corridor.

'Nutcase, nutcase, you're my suitcase,' says Barry, rubbing his hands together. 'I'll be off as well, I think.'

'No, please sit down, Barry!' I bellow from across the room. 'I need to help you.'

'No, no, no, no, no. I'll be fine with that one, I will. I'll be just fine with the suitcase, I will. I will. Be fine. With Will. With Will, the suitcase,' he replies, now standing, and dragging his chair across the room.

'No, please, Barry!' I shout. 'I'm not being rude but—'

'Why am I always last?' asks Susan W., crying, an abrupt shift in her mood.

'You're last because you're fast. And fast ladies make great prostitutes!' shouts Arthur, pointing at her.

This sets her off. She's now weeping uncontrollably.

'Arthur, don't say ... Barry, for the love of God, can you ... I'm just coming, Susan, I won't be ...' I stutter, tripping over my disordered thoughts.

The other elders don't register the sudden commotion. They remain seated in the dining room, staring out of the window at the squirrels.

Tracy storms in, her face red and clammy. She's just repositioned Edith with another carer.

'But I didn't know I'd decided to do that,' says Susan W., trying to fight back tears and compose herself.

'You haven't decided to do anything, Susan. I promise. I promise you're not a prostitute,' I say, crouched down beside her, with my hand on her shoulder.

'You'd struggle to pay the rent, I can tell you that,' says Tracy. 'Pope – I just said—'

'Yeah, I heard you. I'm gonna assist Sylvia with her yogurt,' I reply.

I then rush out of the room, leaving Tracy with the post-breakfast chaos.

'Is that you, Pope?' shouts Sylvia from the armchair in her bedroom.

Whoever assisted her with personal care, and transferred her out of her bed and into her chair, didn't do a very good job. (It was probably Tracy.) Her legs are pulled tight against her chest and, having slid down, she's deprived of lumbar support. Plus, there are no pillows slotted beside her, or along her back, to both act as a buffer between her body and the chair and keep her in an upright position. In her present state, she's at risk of sliding off the leather recliner and onto the floor.

'It's me! It's me! You're an old lady!' I say – or, rather, sing. A spontaneous ditty.

'Don't be stupid,' she replies.

I prop her up with some pillows and brush her hair, which was recently cut into a short, stylish bob. (She has a habit of compulsively scratching her scalp, despite no outward signs of dermatitis or skin irritation.) I then perch on the edge of her bed, ready to assist her.

She's already managed to eat a bowl of cornflakes – but, judging by the spoon on the floor, and the soggy cornflakes that are plastered against her clothes, and the tray, and the chair, she must have tried to eat them with her fingers. This is quite common. We'll even catch her purposely throwing her spoon on the floor. But a new, young carer – who's 'floating' between units – was supposed to assist her with her breakfast (while Tracy turned Edith and I served breakfast in the dining room) to prevent this from happening.

I clear up the mess and wipe down her clothes.

'You'll stay and talk to me, won't you, Pope?'

'Yeah, of course! Do you want your yogurt now as well?'

'Yes. With horseradish sauce.'*

'Not in a yogurt, Sylvia. It'll be horrible.'

'You don't like me much, do you.'

'Of course I do! I love you. You know that. But you won't eat your yogurt if there's horseradish sauce in it. I promise.'

---

* She loves horseradish sauce.

'Ohhh,' she says, like a kid who's just learnt some new information.

'Is horseradish sauce poisonous?' she continues.

'No. You have it all the time. Just not in a yogurt.'

'Ohhh.'

There's a pause.

'Is horseradish sauce and yogurt poisonous?'

'No. It's just not very nice. It goes better with savoury stuff.'

'Ohhh.'

When we get 'stuck in', there's a funereal quality to the conversations I have with Sylvia. They're very death-oriented. Or there'd be a funereal quality to them if they weren't between two people who seem to delight in talking about death.

I've always been eager to announce celebrity deaths to my mum and dad. (My death notices open with 'Guess who's fucking dead?') Plus, a lot of my stand-up material centres on suicide, end-of-life care, etc. (I used to close my set with a protracted death 'scene' in which I hold a bedside vigil for a waning resident and ask, 'Why are you ruining *your* death for *me*?') And Sylvia – with her crypt-keeper bearing, her taloned fingers and witchy face – is preoccupied with what William James calls 'the worm at the core': the awareness of death. I'm only just realising how integral this is to our friendship.

I'm approaching 30. And having reached this point, I've been looking at my life in its totality and reflecting on what I've achieved thus far. Knowing my physical peak was in my mid-twenties, naturally I contemplate whether I utilised – *effectively* utilised – this youthful vigour. Was I adventurous? Did I fling it about? Have I fulfilled my ambitions? Did I find love? I can claim, with a robust certitude, that I absolutely did not do any of this. (Apart from find love. I found it – but she binned it.*)

I drained away my twenties. But working in a care home, among death, and witnessing the essentialism of those final seconds on earth, and how it's the same for everyone, no matter what the circumstances leading up to this moment are – it's levelling and it's clarifying. In death we're all, finally, equal. Therefore it doesn't really matter if so-and-so got on *Mock the Week* despite being an absolute fucking ...

It doesn't matter.

That's the message.

With such an inordinate focus on life's terminus, it might seem counter-productive choosing Sylvia's room to escape the hubbub of the communal areas. How can I relax when death, and life's arbitrariness, is very much in the air?

Normally, as soon as I slip in and perch on the edge of the bed, with Sylvia sitting rigid in her chair, her opalescent eyes swimming in their sockets, trying to locate a more muscular reality than the liquid drift currently in front of her ('Is that you,

---

* The person who's reading this and thinking, *That's about me*. Nah, it's not about you. I can categorically state that it's not about you. It was the one that came after you. Also, can you delete the pictures online where you forced me to style my hair so I looked like a *Yu-Gi-Oh* character? I still go hot and cold with embarrassment thinking about those.

Pope?'), and after she's received confirmation it's me, and as long as she's not in one of her 'body snatcher' moods ('You're not you. I don't believe it for a second. Pope doesn't have a fat voice'), she bombards* me with any of the following questions:

1) Do you believe in hell?
2) Am I in hell?
3) Am I going to die?
4) Am I dead?
5) What does heaven look like?

– and a real curveball –

6) In heaven, will I have to eat my dinner with Mussolini?

Judging by the final question, I'm assuming Sylvia anticipates a provincial, social-realist version of heaven. Carpet and curtains. Golf clubs and women's institutes. People eating dinner and getting 'sozzled' in village halls. But one that retains the same fraught, tentative seating arrangements she's used to in the care home dining room – plus Mussolini. Mussolini, sitting with his knees together, and his eminent chin pushing forward, struggling

---

* 'Bombards' is the wrong word. This version of Sylvia is particularly sweet and inquisitive. Bemused, childlike; wrestling with comprehension. And any questions are asked in a kind of lilting, sing-song way – regardless of what she's enquiring.

with a poached pear. (A bit slides off the spoon. He goes in again; same thing happens. He slams the spoon down onto the table, pushes the bowl to one side and sits with his arms crossed. A carer approaches to offer help, but he waves them away – '*No, grazie*' – and quietly sulks.)

She actually has a whole cache of questions about Mussolini. It's part of her repertoire. And who can blame her? The fumes of Fascism blackened the consciousness of most people who lived through World War Two – but for someone who was married to an Italian it must have been especially carcinogenic.

I've never got a clear picture of her husband. There are no photographs of him in her room. The only information she's passed on is: he was captured by the Americans as a prisoner of war; he was sent to Britain to work on a farm (which is how she came into contact with him); and, when an especially egregious carer (not Tracy this time!) asked her outright if he was a Fascist, she replied, 'Don't be stupid, dear! You're fighting for the country, not the party!' I don't know if that's true under a dictatorship. I don't even know if these tantalising fragments have any historical credibility. She's in her nineties and suffers from delusions. But in other ways, there's a lot of clarity in her thinking – and both her surname and the idle, throwaway recollections from her daughter confirm her husband was, in fact, Italian.

It's an unanswered query that lurks in the background of our companionship: was the husband a blackshirt? Does that make her a collaborationist? Either way, he's proper dead, having passed away many years back. But in the dissociative fantasia of Sylvia's condition – at least when it's at its most pronounced – he'll re-emerge in an intermediate state between life and death. A co-existence. Both here and eating dinner with a stroppy Mussolini. (If Mussolini's there, it's probably not heaven, to be fair.)

'Tell Marco I don't fancy him any more!' Sylvia once announced from a chair in the lounge – a rare foray out of her bedroom.

'Ah, I think ... I think he's gone to the shops, Sylvia,' I replied, part of a provisional dance, or a spinning of plates, as I try to figure out the coordinates of her personal, but forever shifting, reality.

'Who?' she asked.

'Marco,' I replied.

'My husband?'

'Yes.'

'Don't be silly – Marco is dead!'

There was a pause.

'But if you can still tell him I don't fancy him any more, that'd be great. He's waiting for me – by the door frame, there – and I'd rather see what other men are available. Maybe a nice Norwegian.'

Other than through hallucinogenic gateways, or religious practice, I think this is the closest we'll get to catching a glimpse of the interaction between the material and spiritual worlds.

As Leo J. Elders writes in *The Metaphysics of Being of St. Thomas Aquinas in a Historical Perspective*:

Can the past return?* A final question to retain our attention is whether something that has been can return to
existence ... St. Thomas observes that God can do everything which is not contradictory in itself ... Now the past
is that which has been, and it would be a contradiction to
say that it has not been. In reply to the question whether
things which existed formerly can return, Aquinas writes
that natural causes cannot bring this about, as they act
in time and time and movements are now different from

---

* I have a friend I met in university called Richard. He's like an eager
little cartoon dog with a series of machine-gun tics. In between lectures
and seminars, we'd sit in a café (that was conveniently situated next to my
shit university garden) for six hours. Six hours of riffing and pontificating.
Another one of those private salons. Or in his bedroom, where two little
lovebirds called Beth (they were both called Beth) perched on his curtain
rod, flew freely around the room and shat on everything.

After university, he led a peripatetic life, teaching in China and Russia.
(He said he was influenced by – and this always made me piss myself – Jack
Dawson from *Titanic*. Out of all the famous travellers he could have picked!)
Anyway, he vowed to come back into my life every four years and, so far,
he's been true to his word. He'll pop up out of nowhere. The eternal return.

One time we hung out with my demented nan at her house, drinking
beer (not Nan, just us) on a blissful sunny day. We mowed her garden, tidied
up her lounge, opened up the back door to let the Taliban out. And as
Richard and I got progressively more drunk, and Nan pottered around the
house in her usual state of oblivious contentment, we moved closer to Nan's
muddled world. The abstract conversations we had with her started to make
sense. I also remember the London Olympics were on. I think we watched
a bit of the archery. The fact there are these seemingly uneventful days that
you hold in your head and you can't quite discern why they mean so much
to you – it's weird, isn't it.

what they were; hence the same effect numerically will not come back again. But because God's causality is beyond time and change, God can make that a thing which has ceased to be, comes into existence once again.

All the dead spouses, surging through space and time, with temporal spears and thunderbolts of discomforting memory whizzing past them, so they can reluctantly join the shackle that ties them to earth – the husband or wife they thought they'd left behind. And *still* they've forgotten it was the sister-in-law's birthday. Better get a card on the way through the wormhole.

• • •

Sam Keen, in the foreword to an edition of Ernest Becker's seminal work *The Denial of Death*, writes, 'Gradually, reluctantly, we are beginning to acknowledge that the bitter medicine he prescribes – contemplation of the horror of our inevitable death – is, paradoxically, the tincture that adds sweetness to mortality.'

And Dainin Katagiri, in *Returning to Silence: Zen Practice in Daily Life*, attests to the central role in Buddhism of contemplating death: 'Buddhist faith is to live one's life in clarity and purity. Purity is oneness between subject and object; there is no gap between them. Clarity is to gaze at eternity that is no mystery. It is to see human life including death. This is important for us.'

I'd take both of these ideas to such an extreme that – during the periods when I was emptied of any life-enhancing qualities, when I was at my most depleted – I'd actively seek out death on the internet. Beheading videos; shooting rampages; Russian soldiers on their knees, next to a ditch, summarily executed with a bullet to the head; Saddam Hussein being hanged and, for a moment, illuminated by one unbroken ray of light. The deep, red blood. The squeal of anguish escaping from a severed larynx – then the uvular haemorrhage that signals the end of it all. (Maybe there's a final, floating instant as they detach from this world?)

There's something indecent about *choosing* to be a spectator of such brutality. I didn't like it but, after watching these videos, I was aware of the impermanence of everything, the finite nature of degradable matter, including human beings – and the thoughts that might have been going through their soon-to-be lopped-off heads. (Mainly, I presume, *It's pretty mad this is how I die. What a turn-up for the books.*)

Part of me has a morbid fascination with fatality. Bumping up against the finitude of my own mortality, I get a rise – similar to an opiate high.* Though, considering the *permanence* of death (at least in the material realm), this soon gives way to existential anguish and concerns about how Mum would feel if I died prematurely.

---

* This makes me sound mental. I'm not actively seeking death like a storm chaser – rushing into care homes shouting, 'Has it happened? Has she gone? Well, give me a call when her lips turn blue!' But being close to one of the most important and profound events in a person's life has an impact on my body chemistry.

When I'm alone in a room with a person who's dying, it's as if everything shrivels down to the final flickers of contact between us. Whether it's moistening their lips with a swab or holding on to a sinewy hand that's no longer 'body' – only mechanics. You'd expect it to have a profundity of meaning – to be stuffed with moral considerations or thoughts on the metaphysics of the soul – but the contemplation comes *after* the fact. In the room, with the dying elder, in my role as the Ferryman of Essex, it's as if we're outside time. The bureaucratisation of care, and the insistence that we fit everything into a timetable, including end-of-life care – I don't let it encroach on this sacred space. Upper management can go fuck themselves.

But the other side of it is absence. Blankness. And not just the person-as-thing transition that occurs when vital functions have ceased – the lumpen materiality of a 'desouled' cadaver – but also the initial response to the body, and the recognition that this isn't an experience you're sharing with the dead. Even if there's 'conscious survival' – an afterlife, in whatever form that takes – I don't think a post-death consciousness can relate to present life. And when I've been alone in a room with a person who's *just* died, I linger for a moment, and fully *experience* what's going on – and it's empty. It's blank. And it's so incredibly lonely.*

---

* During one of these times, I stood beside the bed, under a dim light, with the cold night air coming in through a crack in the window, feeling the pressure of extreme silence – and to the corpse, I said: 'You're fat.' I don't know why. An internal force coaxed me into saying something at odds with the solemnity of the occasion.

But seeing it does put things into perspective. And I'm aware that using someone else's death as a teachable moment – as an opportunity for personal growth – is pretty disgusting. We have a tendency to use other people as case studies for, say, the perils of addiction. As cautionary tales. Or the atrocities perpetrated against Jewish people and African people to highlight the evils of totalitarianism and imperialism, respectively. That sort of shit.*

There was a lady who died while holding my hand. It happened a few years back. We'll call her Elsie. She'd been out of sorts for the duration of the morning. Sleepy, uncommunicative, barely eating or drinking. She had a wan complexion and was cold to the touch. But none of it was cause for alarm – not for the time being anyway – so Pat made the decision to closely monitor her and asked me to keep an eye on things.

After breakfast we hoisted her into a chair in the conservatory. There was less noise and we could open the door to her left – the one leading to the garden – if she needed fresh air. Also, it was a sunny day and light was streaming in through the windows.

I decided to sit next to her while filling in the nutrition charts, in case her condition rapidly deteriorated. Whenever I asked her how she was, or assisted her with a drink (she only managed sips), she'd give a monosyllabic response – but a response nonetheless.

---

* When I die you can pin me up on a bit of plywood and wheel me out during NA meetings. They can use me as a drug disposal receptacle like the knife bins you see outside police stations.

Another resident's family members had come for a visit and were sitting among the rest of the elders in the lounge. A little girl – approximately eight years old – came to the conservatory and sat in the chair to my right. On my left side, I held Elsie's hand. Even though I was busy with paperwork, I wanted her to know I was still with her, that I was close by, and she could alert me to any changes in her health.

The little girl initiated a conversation:

'Do you like doing what you're doing?' she asked, wide-eyed and inquisitive.

'It's OK,' I replied. 'It's nice to spend time with lots of nans and grandads.'

'Do you stop them poopin'?'

'No. They poop like everyone else.'

'What happens with the poop?'

'It goes in the toilet.'

'Because my nana had a poop in her hand,' she said, giggling.

'That's because some of these nans and grandads are a bit poorly and forget what they're doing. But even though it can be funny, we should try to help them instead of laughing.'

'My nana put the poop on the table and Mummy got cross. But I still love Nana.'

'Yeah, that's good! You should always love her. She doesn't mean any harm.'

'Does Peppa Pig poop in her hand?'

'I don't know.'

At this point I realised Elsie's hand was clinched quite tightly around my own. I turned to my left and gently prodded her shoulder, but I already knew what I was looking at. I pressed the emergency alarm on the nearest control panel and Pat, Ligaya and a couple of other carers arrived after charging down the corridors. (Well. Ligaya and the other carers did. Pat never runs.) The little girl was still in the same chair in the conservatory, playing with a box of yarn and muttering to herself as part of an imaginary game.

The staff who were present gathered in a semi-scrum and had a furtive exchange about the moral quandary we'd found ourselves in. How do we (a) remove a corpse from the conservatory, (b) avoid corrupting an eight-year-old's innocence and (c) preserve the dignity of the deceased?

I hate to say it, but it ended up being a *Weekend at Bernie's* scenario. Due to the prying eyes of those congregated in the lounge, we pretended Elsie was sick, lifted her into a wheelchair and went to transfer her to her bedroom.

'Has she got tummy ache?' asked the little girl.

'Yeah, a little bit of that,' I replied.

'Has she got headache?' she continued.

'I think it's only tummy ache,' I replied.

'Has she got—'

'She feels sick and she's had enough questions from little girls!' interrupted Pat.

And as we wheeled her away, Pat – under her breath – said, 'The poor cow is dead, now piss off into the garden.'

In Elsie's bedroom we lifted her out of the wheelchair and onto the bed – while being careful to unbend, and straighten, her already rigid body. This was followed by the usual post-evacuation ablution ritual. (Once the fluids have emptied from the person's 'carapace' – from the material body – we wash and dress them in the same way we would if they were alive. One notable difference – other than the eeriness of a waxy, lifeless body – is the deep, subterranean stench.)

Now – in the same way I believe we should familiarise ourselves with bodily abjection, we shouldn't create distance between the individual and their understanding of finitude. And if we were acquainted with, in the words of Thomas Nagel, 'the unequivocal and permanent end of our existence' from an early age – we could avoid what happened to Elsie and stop erecting partitions for our children.

Maybe I, too, have a partial aversion to death. If so, watching online gore when I was younger would have been my way of overcompensating – or reaffirming that death happens and I'm not indestructible.

My death-oriented perspective manifests itself – as in other areas of my life – as a childish undermining of death; as irreverence. But, ultimately, catheterising circumstance and temporarily draining it of its misery is what works for me. Irreverently hooting at the reaper – and then dulling the pain with drugs because I'm unable to process my grief like a grown-up. Or I used to be anyway. That method is no longer available to me – clean and serene – so I'm forced to sit with my grief.

But I have to acknowledge that it's easy for me to react like this (the jokes, the stuff about the 'healing potential of a dark comic sensibility') because I've never been slashed open, and turned inside out, tender organs whipped by gales, sending a raw-nerve tremor through my being – I've never been reduced to this by the grief of a significant death.

Is this even an accurate estimation of what grief, and then deep mourning, feels like? Or is it impoverished, muted and nothing; a punishing absence?

A bit of both, I imagine. Like a row of snails on an old brick wall – and one suddenly bursting in wicked triumph after being shot with a BB gun. But the scanning eye resumes its course, and it's apathetic snails for the remaining length of the wall. Though at any moment – when you remember who's gone away – the trigger could be pulled again. *That's* what I imagine the first phase of grief to be like.

The closest I've come to experiencing significant grief was when my dog, Dave, passed away. I know it's not comparable, and I know some people will think I'm minimising the death of a human being, but he was a constant presence during my lonely college years, when I'd stay up all night, sitting in my lounge, anxious about spending another day at the edges of the college social scene (where I'd privately hype myself up to initiate conversations with other students – always stumbling at the last minute). Dave was always there, lying next to me, with bunched-up rolls of fat on his neck and weird Paul Hollywood eyes. He was neutered but over-sexed, so, more often than not, he had a boner that seemed to confuse him. Ah, nostalgia.

But since working in care, my interest in death, or the Grand Guignol that precedes death, has been heightened – though, surprisingly, I haven't experienced a lot of grief. The thing is, our relationships with the residents start at a point of decline. We're always anticipating the slippage between dying and death because, even if a resident is relatively 'intact', they're in the home because they're shedding health, and they're discarding the total independence that comes with optimal health.

'Dementia is a particularly long farewell to the self,' writes Nicci Gerrard in *What Dementia Teaches Us about Love*.

With most illnesses, death comes quite quickly. With dementia, the flicker with which life ends is excruciatingly slowed. People who live with it may have plenty of time to contemplate their own going; their carers have even longer, often many years of imagining and preparing and rehearsing. There's an anticipated, ambiguous grief, a premature mourning of the self, or of the beloved other.

But seeing a resident's family members reckon with the dissolution of their relationship, it makes me anxious about my own parents dying – whether by sudden death or a gradual fade-out – and being left alone in the world. What the fuck would I do then?

Who would talk to me about worms and anencephalic babies? Who will call me out for gaining weight?

I'd be sitting in the lounge – a lounge I've been sitting in since they brought me into this world – but, this time, with no one to listen to me bang on about things they don't care about. Man, it just hit me. The realisation that, one day, it'll be a reality. That one day I'll be living that loneliness. That one day they'll be gone.

Fuck.

It's too much to take.

· · ·

I went through a stage of fucking up my face to release the valve on internal pressures. The first time I gave myself a black eye was in the care home during a shift. It was an extemporaneous act, spur of the moment. I had a slight black eye from a fight I'd had in Romford – and I started 'topping it up' throughout the day. A couple of swift jabs at regular intervals. And when I was doing it, it seemed totally casual, a fun little project to be getting on with. Like I was covering a Coke can with plumbing tape.

My colleagues couldn't understand the sudden acceleration of the bruising and the swelling. My eye, over the duration of a seven-hour shift, went from having a mild purpling around the socket to being this heavy, bulging plum, too distended for me to open. I blamed it on a delayed reaction.

At the time I was in a fraught relationship that was (to severely diminish the psychic toll it had on both of us) a bit of a ball ache. And I was stressed out at work. A week prior to this, a resident had fallen ill. I don't remember much about the woman in question, other than that she reminded me of a pencil. She was slender and chinless, narrow-shouldered, with little definition in her face. I feel awful I can't provide her with the sinew and fibre of an accurate character representation, that I can't bring her to life. I've cared for so many people over the years, an entire cruise ship of lost souls who needed protecting from the flood of their failing consciousness.

There are some you can recall in an instant. Too big to ignore. Your Hatties. Your Arthurs. There are some who become surrogate nans and grandads. Family members. Intimates. For me, Sylvia is one of those.

It's now 8pm in the care home. There's a film of grease on my nose, forehead and cheeks. And because I haven't had a chance to drink anything for a few hours, my mouth tastes like bins.

Since this morning there have been the usual trials and tribulations. After bathing Susan W., I sprayed too much deodorant, which she inhaled, causing her to vomit all over me – luckily I'd draped a towel over my shoulder as I was about to dry her, which caught the worst of it.

I got into a big argument with Tracy about her continuous smoking breaks – which would have been forgivable if she also took Ed out with her. (The poor bloke's been patiently waiting – though indiscreetly hovering – in anticipation of a carer who can escort him.)

And Dorothy tried to eat a novelty playing card with a picture of Telly Savalas on it.

For now, everything is sorted. Paperwork done; clinical waste taken to the yellow bins; cups of tea offered and distributed to residents who are still awake; two-hourly turns and pad changes completed. It's the final golden hour. As Ed's in his room, and Ethel's in bed, rather than in the lounge, I decide to check on Sylvia.

She's in bed, with her eyes closed, but muttering to herself.

'Am I in hell?' she asks, as soon as I step into the room.

'Good hearing, Sylvia!' I say.

'Is that you, Pope?'

'Yes, it's me,' I reply, sluggishly.

It's been a long day. Mentally I'm winding down.

'How's your mother?' Sylvia asks, the start of her roll call of questions.

'She's fine. Nothing to report.'

There's a pause.

'Would you be sad if I died?' she asks.

'Yes, of course!' I reply.

I would. She's one of the few residents I'll mourn – *properly* mourn – when she passes. It's not that I don't love or feel affection towards the other residents. It's just you become jaded to the terminal prognosis, the palliative care, the multitudinous dead. And then there's the financial imperative of filling the recently vacated rooms as quickly as possible. You're not given time to acclimatise. One in, one out. And usually I'd think of it as the natural course of things but, of course, it's not natural. The absence of rites or a ceremonial passing-over directly preceding the event isn't natural. Even elephants have those! But in care homes, death is nothing but an administrative duty – another task to be ticked off the list. And maybe *that's* why there's surprisingly little grief among carers? But when Sylvia dies, and they shove another person in this room, to me it'll be like an invasion, an improper encroachment on Sylvia's home.

But, as I say, not every person I've cared for looms large in my memory. There are vague figures, apparitions, with a semblance of facial expression or idiosyncratic behaviour. But the moment my brain reaches forward, they crumble into a heap of ash and get carried off by the breeze.

And there are some who are just a pencil.

They exist as nothing more.

But the reason this woman – who died a week before I started giving myself black eyes – was so notable was the sequence of events that led to her hospital admission and eventual death.

This was years ago now, in one of the first care homes I ever worked in. She was a shuffler, a dodderer, but liked to keep moving. One day, despite already being quite wan, her complexion sickened, going from grey to green. We encouraged her to lie down on her bed so we could observe her for a couple of hours, and though she was initially resistant, she soon became too weak to agitate against this decision.

As she stared vacantly at the faces hovering over her, or the shadows dancing across her plain white ceiling, she developed a bubbling, a whistling, in her throat, and I urged the CTM on shift to ring an ambulance.

'No, not yet. Keep an eye on her,' was her response.

I was slightly timorous as a carer then because I was still so new to the job – and only working part-time as I was at university. I didn't yet have the years of experience that would lend me any authority (though that's not necessarily a reliable gauge of good practice). Still, a few of us were uncomfortable with this, and – in our guts – it seemed like a dereliction of duty.

'What's happening with this woman – it's isn't right,' said one of the other junior carers, a grave portentousness withering the atmosphere in the room.

I kept checking on her.

She was responsive but, since she was quite a laconic woman, it was hard to determine much via verbal communication. To me, it was obvious she was struggling to breathe. There was an encroaching note of urgency in our appeals to the manager. She hesitated before making up her mind: no phoning an ambulance. (And knowing this particular manager, I'd say it was motivated by social awkwardness, or a reluctance to deal with difficult situations, rather than any firm conviction.)

I was watching a woman consumed with a quiet panic that she was unable to understand. And when I visited her room, she'd look to where I was standing, the bubbling becoming more abrasive, like the twist of a salt mill – and her eyes were pleading. I'm sure of it. I wasn't projecting. But the manager said I had to assist the other residents and that all my attention couldn't be concentrated on one person.

I wasn't aware of procedural matters like 'Get everything in writing', so as my shift was finishing, I accepted the assurances from the manager that the ambulance would be called. This woman *needed* help.

But for now, I'd done as much as I could. (Hadn't I?)

I was able to go home with a clean conscience. (Wasn't I?)

When I returned three days later – she was still there. Same clothes. Same position. Lacquered with a deathly lividity. I couldn't fucking believe it.*

A different manager was on shift this time ('What is wrong with that woman? Why didn't she deal with this? This woman looks like a bloody Twiglet!'), and instantly phoned for an ambulance.

The paramedics arrived, a bustle of medicalised activity, and commenced the elaborate choreography of first-responder ballet along with the semaphore of hospital jargon – always bamboo-zling, mystifying and intimidating. And always a source of contention among carers, who feel belittled by them. But on this

* I was younger, and far less confident as a care worker. I didn't know how to question what was happening or lodge a formal complaint. Mainly, I was reluctant to take it on as my own cause because there was a lot of misinformation surrounding this and I didn't know who to trust. The most diabolical part is that events like this just seem to go away. There never seems to be repercussions if an elderly person is involved.

occasion, they rightfully excoriated us for letting her get in this state. 'Three days?! She's been like this for three days?!'

(The new manager, for all her righteousness, managed to slip out and avoid a bollocking. 'I need to just get ... you're alright with this, Pope?' she said as she was leaving. I absorbed it. I absorbed the recriminations. And when I skulked out of the room, my head held in shame, I found her just standing in the corridor, looking at the wall. As the paramedics filtered out with the resident on a stretcher, she quickly scarpered around the corner.)

The woman was in hospital for two days before dying an anxious death.

It haunted me then and it haunts me still. And I was complicit because I should have fought harder or called the ambulance myself. I should have checked up in the intervening days between shifts.

I was wracked with a penalising guilt, and I took it out on myself. I gave myself hefty black eyes as if I were de-weeding the driveway, emerging from the toilet with my sleeves rolled up. A job well done. 'That's self-flagellation off the checklist! Time for lunch.'

I didn't know this woman was dying. No one was consciously leaving a woman to die. But thankfully that – out of nine years of care work – is the only time I've witnessed a *drastic* failing.

'Death will be full of surprises,' writes Sallie Tisdale in *Advice for the Dying: A Practical Perspective on Death.*

Tibetan Buddhists practice dying through special meditations and visualisations, so that they will recognise the experience when it happens and not be caught off guard. They think of death as a long process, beginning before the body ceases to function and unfolding over days, weeks, even years. Tibetan Buddhism teaches that immediately after death, a person enters the so-called bardo planes, intermediate states after death and before rebirth.

If Pencil is in the bardo – 'the entire braid of the self [having come] unwound in a rush' – and there's any way for me to communicate with her over that threshold (maybe she's eating dinner with Mussolini? Maybe she's walking Dave over glistening, celestial gardens, occasionally telling him off because of his unruly boner?) I'd like to say: I'm sorry. I'm sorry I didn't do better by you. And I'm sorry I can't remember your name. You deserve more.

And, for the moment, I'll relinquish the opportunity to make a joke.

Unless you're up for it?

EPILOGUE

The man is sitting on the lip of the stage with his legs dangling over the edge, his feet a few centimetres from the floor. This is where he usually ends up, going from standing, to sitting, to kneeling, before arriving at his final resting position, having substituted the stool for the stage and shunned the static spotlight.

He's in the gloom, close to the carpet (a carpet that smells of sweat and stale beer). He listlessly holds the microphone and, with the other hand, picks up a small piece of broken glass and rolls it between his fingers.

He has flushed, shiny cheeks. His beard has become slick and dense, like an otter's pelt. He continues to tug at his sweatshirt to free it from his belly crevice. The woodlouse has made its way to the stool's surface. They're the only things currently illuminated. Well, those and the dust that drifts through the cone of light. And the tip of the man's head as it occasionally peeks out of the darkness.

The voice emanating from the speaker sounds disembodied – but still loud and boisterous. It hits right inside the ear. But you can detect a weariness in it.

It's late.

It's humid.

He's tired.

He's almost done.

'Remember when I quit a fourteen-hour shift only three hours in? That's how I quit my job as a carer.'

* * *

There wasn't a definitive event that forced me out. I'd been mentally circling the drain for a while – and even though management wanted to hold on to me for as long as possible, they understood my reasons.* And the problem was a lot larger than just the care homes I've worked in. There's a fatal disregard for the

---

* I didn't book myself into a hotel this time. It took me a week to even tell my family I'd left. Like Jean-Claude Romand – a French mythomaniac who murdered his wife and children – I pretended to go to work, with my water bottle and packed lunch, and sat on trains or buses or walked through the broken ruins of places like Hadleigh Castle. I even joined a bowls league.

entire enterprise of social care. One that won't be remedied by a £36 billion tax levy.*

The problems with social care are too fundamental, long-running and deep.

'The aim is to give people a good life, a happy life, not a paternalistic service to passive recipients,' said former care minister Norman Lamb when asked about social care reform on *Newscast*. But in all the debates on social care that have been aroused by the pandemic, the *quality* of care – care that leads to a good, happy life, rather than the simple continuation of it – hasn't been prioritised in any of the government's messaging.

Luckily I had my comedy income to fall back on – until the pandemic ballsed that up.

●　●　●

---

* In September 2021, Boris Johnson's government announced a 1.25 per cent national insurance tax increase for working adults to fund a 'catch-up programme' for the NHS and 'reform the adult social care sector'. On the subject of the latter, according to the press release, 'The system will finally be reformed, ending unpredictable and catastrophic care costs faced by thousands, and making the system fairer for all.' However, whether social care receives any of this money is contingent on the NHS clearing the Covid backlog; only then will the funds trickle down. Given the unprecedented pressure on the NHS in the past two years and the drastic need for recruitment and higher wages in the health care sector, will there really be anything left for those who live or work in care homes?

I'm not going to pretend this is a definitive report on life in care homes, or as a care worker, or anything more than a deeply personal and idiosyncratic account of my experience on the frontline of minimum-wage employment, and by a druggy narrator who (temporarily) departed the social body and found friends – friends with broken brains* – in the hot box that is the care home.

But I hope there's a recognisable universality to some of my experiences or the day-to-day portrait of working in these environments. To me, it's important to portray care homes as they come – including the parts of them that are messy and inconvenient. Maybe it'll change the culture and some of the dehumanising practices brought about by systemic failings. And maybe it'll force us to confront the innate dis-comfort we have with illness and ageing and allow us to relinquish shame – whether it's personal shame or shame on a relative's behalf.

Emotions are never stable – especially when you're chasing a high that, in the long run, always eludes you – but, ultimately, I loved those elders and cared for them the best I could. But as it currently stands, the psychic and physical toll of being a care worker isn't sustainable. And no matter how many times the care providers fill their employment brochures with

---

* And burst dicks and awkward choreography and speech refracted through a spoliating consciousness.

soft-focus photographs of smiling carers, with smiling residents, and sunlight pouring in through the window, it isn't the *good* life that Norman Lamb said we should be aiming for.

There's a dearth of resources and – because care homes are for-profit businesses – the providers are operating on extremely thin profit margins. Overstretched staff, consumed by stress and anxiety, in the dust cloud of a frantic schedule, being paid so little that they're unable to put away money for their *own* future care needs – these aren't the kind of people who'll cultivate communality and collective effervescence among the residents. Instead they'll retire to the staff toilet and pop a couple of Xanax in between rounds of stoma bag drainage.

• • •

During a family trip around north-eastern USA and Canada – a trip undertaken a couple of months after I quit my job; a trip where, as a cost-cutting initiative, I shared hotel rooms with my parents and slept in baths lined with coats – I spent the evenings traversing streets and spotlit parks or sitting in bars and diners in whatever city we happened to be in.

In Philadelphia, underneath a highway overpass, I sat beside a shelter constructed from damp cardboard and spoke to its occupant. He showed me a deep, cavernous wound on his thigh that, at various points in the conversation, was caused by either a shotgun or diabetes. And he seemed intent on getting me to sandwich-bag my hand so I could dip it into the ulcer to prove how deep it was. *

'I'll probably just take your word for it, mate, but thank you for the offer,' I said, so as not to be impolite.

And in New York, while loafing on a bench beside the Hudson River, I was joined by a tall, Lurch-like Romanian jogger wearing a white vest, basketball shorts and a do-rag. After fifteen minutes of congenial small talk (he used to be a realtor), he pulled out his phone and showed me a video of a limbless torso bobbing on the water, butting up against the edge of the walkway, in the exact spot we were facing.

'That's where I found it,' he said, with a big grin on his face, and then played the local news report of the incident.

I made my excuses and hastily parted ways, but as I walked along a darkened underpass on my way back to the hotel, I grabbed a small discarded rocking horse in case I needed a weapon – only for a group of rowdy teenagers to kick it out of my hands and stomp it to bits.

Other than that – lovely city!

The only reason I mention this is because among the other holiday highlights (accidentally witnessing a person on all fours presenting their anus† to a group of Koreans playing basketball, anyone?), I was compelled to help an elderly stranger wearing

---

* Imagine reaching a point in your life where all you've got left is bragging rights on wound depth.

† It's quite an anus-heavy book, isn't it.

jogging bottoms drenched in urine – so much so that the weight of them had dragged the waistband to halfway down the man's thighs.

It was in Boston. And I offered assistance because my conscience kept snagging on the sight of this man pinballing between unaffected pedestrians – or those who looked him up and down, and organised their face to convey an adequate level of concern, but didn't act on it.

I saw him from a distance, but when I finally caught up with him and offered my help, he told me it often happened, and he seemed resigned to the fact that, when it did, he had to sit on a bench until he was dry enough to be allowed back on public transport. And this is what happens when civic-mindedness has depleted and social responsibility is replaced with the prioritisation of individual well-being; the right to ignore the pissy man so the spectator can remain uncontaminated by his abjection.

I bought him some spare jogging bottoms and walked him to a public toilet, where I waited outside to give him his privacy. And when he emerged and he'd changed into the fresh pair, I helped him to tie up the soiled clothing in a plastic bag. Finally, I sat with him at his bus stop and he regaled me with stories about the Vietnam War.*

If there's anything to take away from this book it's an unshakeable belief in my saintliness. Why else would I include

---

* I could have done with a bit less of his bangin' on if I'm being totally honest with myself.

such an anecdote in the closing paragraphs? But putting aside the implicit self-sanctification of any 'I Help People' memoir – and putting aside the moral slipperiness of such a project – I hope the population pays closer attention to the social care sector. I hope people are better equipped to deal with illness and ageing, and are able to see dementia as something more than an obliteration-in-slow-motion.

I also hope I can convince readers to send an email offering to volunteer at a local care home and commit to doing a 'shift' every week or month. Maybe this will broaden the support for wage increases, better training and more resources for the care home employees. And, most important of all, I hope I've raised my profile enough that I can sell out a 50-seater venue like this [the man waves his hand over the empty chairs in front of him]. Then on my next pay day I won't have to visit a cashpoint at 3am to withdraw all the money to prevent it from being swallowed by overdue bank charges. And finally – finally! – I'll be able to afford that tattoo of a cat with tits.

Laters!

PS. I've kept diaries/journals/notebooks since I was six years old. The placeholder title for this book was 'Old Knobs', but since the editors had reservations about marketing a book called 'Old Knobs' I had to look for an alternative. I looked through the journals from the correct time period – one had a still from Ingmar Bergman's 'Persona' sellotaped onto the cover; one had

'ACAB = All Cops Are Beans' in embossed, label-maker lettering stuck along the spine – and came across a transcript of a conversation I had with an old lady who was happily waiting to die:

OL: 'Am I dying today?'

PL: 'No, not yet! And hopefully not any time soon. I need someone to talk to!'

OL: 'So, not today then?'

PL: 'No. Not today. Plus, you have bingo before lunch.'

OL: 'Oh, good. Well, maybe – maybe I'll die after bingo.'

PL: (*Laughing*) 'Perfect end to a perfect morning.'